WHAT A COINCIDENCE!

It's the stories we tell that define us.

LARRY PROCTOR

◆ FriesenPress

Suite 300 - 990 Fort St
Victoria, BC, V8V 3K2
Canada

www.friesenpress.com

Copyright © 2021 by Larry Proctor
First Edition — 2021

All rights reserved.

While all of the anecdotes in this book are true stories, some of the names associated with them have been changed.

No part of this publication may be reproduced in any form, or by any means, electronic or mechanical, including photocopying, recording, or any information browsing, storage, or retrieval system, without permission in writing from FriesenPress.

ISBN
978-1-03-911668-9 (Hardcover)
978-1-03-911667-2 (Paperback)
978-1-03-911669-6 (ebook)

1. Biography & Autobiography, Personal Memoirs

Distributed to the trade by The Ingram Book Company

Table of Contents

Introduction	1
What a Coincidence!	3
Larry Street	5
Determination	7
Before the Remote	8
Are You my Type?	11
Confidence	13
A Letter to Mr. Ballard	15
Roller Coaster or Merry-Go-Round?	19
The Multi-purpose Essay	19
I Deserve an Extra Mark	21
Dear Mr. Bassett	23
The Summer Job Interview	27
The New Career Interview	27
Welcome to Nassau	31
Toilet Training	35
My Sister, the Boy	35
Tomorrow's Leaders	37
Tracking Down the Culprit	39
Revenge on the Noisy Neighbors	43
A Daughter's Love at a Convenient Time	45
A Son's Love at a Convenient Time	45
Career Ambitions	45
Café de Soir	47
Con Job	49
Little Things (about me) that Bug my Wife	53
New Words	53
The "N" Word	55
The Senior's Shopping List	57
The Roommate	59
The Accident	63
The Glass is Not Empty	67

Preparation for the Real World	*69*
One Way Conversation	*71*
The Conditioned Response	*72*
Run to Me	*73*
No Privacy Here	*75*
Where's the Rest of my Pay?	*79*
Mr. Bean?	*81*
Cat Fight	*83*
The Frosh	*85*
Elevator Ride	*86*
Sewer Stories	*87*
That's Covered by Insurance, Right?	*91*
Now, What do I do?	*93*
A Bend in the arm	*95*
Roger for Coach	*97*
Why We Are Who We Are	*101*
The Not-So-Amazing Race	*103*
On Stage Alone, in Front of a Crowd	*105*
The Raid	*107*
More Activities of the Leaders of Tomorrow	*111*
Snow Wall & Santa's Rough Day	*113*
Oh, my Deer!	*115*
Telemarketers	*117*
The Second Time Around Interview	*119*
Job Search	*121*
Oh, Christmas Tree	*125*
Quotes by People I Know	*127*
Progressive Dinners	*129*
Home Signs	*131*
What Kind of Fruit are You?	*133*
Fight or Flight	*135*
Mind Games	*137*
DENSA	*139*
Strike!	*141*
Travel	*143*

The Leafponaut	*145*
The Hockey Coach	*147*
Performance Evaluation	*149*
The Effective Meeting	*151*
The Dummy Who Made us Money	*153*
A Letter to my Sister	*157*
Just Another Coincidence	*161*
The Proposal	*163*
I Would Like to Marry your Daughter	*165*
The Mighty Duck Influence	*167*
Gidget the Dog	*169*
The Ombudsman	*171*
Winner's Circle	*175*
50 Things I've learned about My Wife	*177*
Another Difficult Decision	*179*
The Dream	*181*
Spell Check	*183*
Sometimes, There's Nothing You Can Do	*185*
The Snowball Letter	*187*
A Child's Definition of "Budget"	*189*
Surprise Me	*191*
Toothy Art	*195*
Bedtime	*197*
More Alike Every Day	*199*
The Christmas Newsletter	*201*
Your Favorite Films	*203*
Powerful Image	*205*
Now I Understand	*205*
Longevity	*207*
What Does the Future Hold?	*211*
Conclusion	*213*

*This book is dedicated
to my family,
Margaret, Jeremy & Laura.*

Introduction

Have you ever heard someone recount a personal story or incident and have it remind you of something similar you have experienced? It happens to me all the time.

When a group of friends get together, that's invariably what tends to take place. One discussion leads to another, some stories are worth remembering; some are likely to be retold many times in the future; others are forgotten almost as soon as they end. You may even wonder how you ever got onto a particular topic and then trace back the links.

There are times when someone may ask a question and listen to the answers of others, but all they really wanted to do was tell their own story. Rather than just launching into it or stating their opinion, it would seem a better idea to ask others for theirs first.

The 1994 movie Forrest Gump, which starred Tom Hanks, is a story of a very simple man who ends up leading what could be termed an extraordinary life. The film opens with a camera shot of a feather being blown around high in the sky. After a number of twists and turns, it eventually comes down to earth, landing at the feet of Forrest who is sitting on a park bench.

He is talking to whoever happens to be sitting next to him at the time. They change over the course of the movie. He reflects on his life, a life that included a childhood rife with ridicule due to a physical impairment. However, it was also a life where he goes on to meet celebrities such as Elvis Presley; becomes a college football star; fights in the Vietnam War and then protests against that same war; meets a president of the United States; starts a business that looks like a big blunder; sees that same business become very profitable; and in the end sees himself as nothing more than the simple man that he is.

The movie shows a person who does things without much rhyme or reason. At times he unwittingly inspires others to follow him. Then, just as quickly as he chose one course in life, he stops and moves on to something else. Along the way he makes new friends, loses others and sees some endure forever.

There was no predominant theme or direction to Forrest Gump's life. It was merely a series of experiences that in the end collectively defined him. Throughout the film, he often repeats what his mother told him, "Life is like a box of chocolates. You never know what you're going to get."

At the end of the movie, the camera begins to pull away from him as he sits on another bench, seeing his young son off to school. A gust of wind picks up that same feather and blows it skyward. It's tossed back and forth, to and fro, going higher and higher, its direction and final destination unknown, much like the life of Forrest Gump.

We all collect a number of experiences throughout our lives that in some way define us as individuals. They won't necessarily be noteworthy or remarkable in any way, but they might be interesting or amusing. Some may be unique and some may even be thought-provoking. Others will seem like strange coincidences.

This book is a collection of anecdotes. They appear randomly, reflecting what is sometimes the seemingly randomness of our lives. Some of the stories are personal and others were conveyed by friends and family. Ideally, they may inspire readers to recall their own personal experiences and to consider how their lives may have been shaped by them, however modest or unassuming that may be.

I hope that by reading the stories that follow, you will reflect on some of your own.

What a Coincidence!

I first met George Proctor when I was President of the Caledon East Softball Association. He was organizing a family function of some sort and wanted to arrange a fun game of softball at the local ball park as part of the occasion. We lent him some equipment and when he came to pick it up, he told me a story of coincidence, a Proctor family story, both his and mine.

Despite sharing the same last name and living within a few miles of each other, George and I were not related, nor were our families.

George had moved to the Caledon area from Toronto a short time earlier and he decided to invite an elderly friend of his from the city to visit. The friend was not familiar with this part of the country, but George gave him detailed directions, a date and time were set and the visit was planned.

"Drive north out of the city and take Highway #50 to Old Church Road. Turn left and drive west to the first road, turn left again and continue driving until you cross the railroad tracks. After crossing the tracks, go to the fourth house on the right. It's a white house with a black roof. We'll see you next Sunday!"

The elderly friend set out on his journey and followed the directions well, at least he followed them well until he got onto Old Church Road. At that point, rather than turning left at the first road he came to (an unpaved country road at the time), he continued driving until he came to what was the first set of traffic lights at the time and also the first paved road. That is where he made his left turn.

This in fact had taken him to the village of Caledon East. He proceeded to follow the remaining directions flawlessly. He passed over a set of railroad tracks, went to the fourth house on the right, which just happened to be a white house with a black roof! What a coincidence! It also happened to be my grandparent's house, last name Proctor. Another coincidence!

The friend parked his car in the driveway, went to the front door and knocked. An unfamiliar face (my grandmother) answered the door. The visitor was now a little puzzled since he did not recognize this lady and it definitely wasn't his friend George Proctor. The visitor asked hesitantly, "Is this the Proctors?"

My grandmother replied, "Yes, it is."

Still puzzled as to who this lady was, but feeling a little relieved that he had found the Proctor's house, the gentleman asked, "Is George home?"

And now for the third coincidence of this story, my grandfather had a brother named George, so my grandmother's response quite naturally was, "George, oh no, George died several years ago!"

"What do you mean he died? I just spoke to him last week!"

In the end the poor fellow found the George Proctor that he had set out to visit, but for a while there, both he and my grandmother were more than a little confused!

Larry Street

Yes, my name is Larry and yes, I do live on Larry Street, but this is in no way a coincidence. It's true. The street I live on is named after me.

I might be completing some sort of application. I might be providing my name and address after making a purchase. Someone may have simply asked me where I live. And then the question or comment will follow. "You live on Larry Street? I bet it's named after you."

Most times I just nod and smile, anxious to move on, but occasionally I say, "Yes, as a matter of fact it is named after me" and I tell them the story.

My grandfather was a farmer. As he gradually eased into retirement in the 1950s, he began to sell subdivided lots from his farm. This meant he was responsible for building the access roads to those lots. The local township, as was the custom at the time, allowed him to name them.

It was 1955 and there were four roads that my grandfather had the privilege of naming. He decided to name two of them after his two daughters-in-law (Jean, my mother and Marion, my aunt). The road that ran from east to west across the top of the hill, he named Hilltop Drive and since I happened to be the only grandchild born at the time, I was fortunate to have the fourth street named after me, Larry Street, in the Town of Caledon.

It starts at Airport Road, runs west, begins to curve to a southerly direction where it meets and ends at Hilltop Drive. It's your typical, nondescript small town street.

I ended up buying a house on Larry Street twenty-eight years later. I looked at some others, but this one was pretty much what I was looking for and if you have the opportunity to live on a street that's named after you, you take it!

Dana Avenue?

Before having children, my mother had decided that if she had a girl, the name would be Diane and if it was a boy, she wanted to name the baby Dana.

"You've got to be kidding," my Dad said. "Dana is a girl's name!" My Dad won the argument and when I was born, I was christened Larry.

Thank you, Dad!

Imagine, I could have been living on Dana Avenue!

Determination

Jeremy had just been moved from a crib to a regular bed. He was less than two years old and the move became necessary for safety's sake. He had found a way to get out of his crib and we, as parents, couldn't figure out how he was doing it. He wasn't tall enough to throw his leg over the side and ease himself down. He wasn't strong enough to pull himself up using arm strength alone. So how did he do it?

One night we passed by his bedroom door at the right time to observe and finally learn his secret. There was a dresser close enough to his crib that was the right height for him to reach with one leg from inside his crib. Once he was able to do that, he was agile enough to push himself onto the dresser and from there shimmy down to the floor below. So, the freedom parents know after putting their kids in a crib in the evening was over for us. No longer could we put our son to bed and know he was there for the night.

Getting your child to go to bed at night and stay there is a problem that many parents encounter. Now that Jeremy was out of the crib and in a real bed, **he** decided **he** would determine when his bedtime was, while I as a parent thought that was **my** call. So, the battle of wills began; a determined father and an equally determined son.

Establishing a routine and some rules, and then following them consistently was the way to go! That's what all the parenting books say, right? So, when Jeremy decided he would get out of bed immediately after I put him there for the night, I picked him up and put him right back! No words were spoken.

Jeremy got out of bed again and I put him back again. He got out a third time and I put him back a third time. The battle of wills continued, each of us determined in our own way to emerge the winner. Occasionally

I'd be able to make my way back downstairs and sit down for a minute or two before he would be up again. Other times he was hot on my heels and ran by me before I was even outside of his bedroom.

The good news is the father finally won, seventy-six put-backs later. Seventy-six times I put my son to bed that night before he finally stayed and fell asleep. (I also fell asleep a short time later).

I'm not sure why I actually counted the number of times I put him to bed, but I did. I assume it was for comparative purposes, perhaps to prove a point when the next evening rolled around.

As it turned out, the following night was more of the same, I'd put Jeremy to bed, he'd get up. I'd put Jeremy back in his bed and he'd get up again. This time my workout ended after fifty-four put-backs.

The third night, the magic number was down to nineteen. The fourth night I had it down to four and finally on the fifth night my son stayed in his bed the first and only time I put him there. I had won! The father was more determined than the son! Well, for this one time anyway.

Okay, so to be honest I can't say that the whole problem never arose again, because I'm sure it did, but a point was made and my wife and I tended to have a wee bit more quiet time to ourselves in the evenings from that day on, or at least until our kids became teenagers.

Before the Remote

Is this story related to the one above? You decide.

I guess Todd was much more likely to take directions from his father as a child than many kids. It's a father/son story. So, that's how it's related.

It was in the days before the television remote control. Todd's dad liked to flip channels, especially during commercials, but he didn't like to get out of his chair to do so. Todd was instructed to sit on a stool beside the television. Whenever his father got bored with what he was watching, he would shout out "Channel 3!" and Todd would obediently turn the dial to channel 3. Some of us are old enough to remember the knob on the tv that was turned to change channels, as opposed to the remote control we have now.

What A Concidence!

"Channel 6!" his dad shouted. Todd turned the dial to the requested station again. I'm not sure how long Todd had to sit on that stool changing channels, but I can't imagine he enjoyed it.

By the way, to make things even more difficult, the large knob that would have been easy to turn to change channels was missing from the family television! Todd had to use a pair of pliers to turn the dial!

Are You my Type?

I always remember my blood type.

A lot of people have trouble recalling what type they are, I guess because it's not something that they're asked very often. I think I know more people who can remember their Social Insurance Number than their blood type.

The first time I donated blood was when I was in university. There was a clinic nearby and some of the other guys in the student residence who had donated previously convinced me to tag along. Everything went well. Afterwards, I was given a card that showed my name and blood type, I had my juice and cookies and felt good about doing something charitable, something I'd probably do again sometime.

Many of the people helping at the blood donor clinics were volunteers, having chosen this as a way they could give back to society. Some, you could tell were confident and had a calmness about them that was reassuring for any of the donors who were a little bit apprehensive about the whole process. Others were not as polished and seemed somewhat nervous themselves. It was this latter type, a retired senior, who checked me in for my second donation, which came about six months after my first.

She examined my donation card, the one with my personal information on it and said, "So, your name is A. Pos."

"Have a seat Mr. Pos and we'll be right with you."

I was relieved to discover her duties were restricted to registration and that she would not be the one sticking any needles in me.

"A Positive", that's my blood type, not my name! I've never forgotten it since!

Fast Forward 30 Years

I'm about to donate blood. The phlebotomist, who hasn't actually stuck the needle in me yet, starts talking to her colleague who is looking after the donor beside me. The colleague comes up by my side and starts stroking my forearm. She tells me I have great veins, easy to locate. I'm not sure if she's used that line on any other guys or not. It's the only specific body part of mine I've ever been complimented on!

I also learned that menopausal women are the worst. Their veins are tough to find.

Phlebotomists really love guys like me. We make their jobs so much easier!

Confidence

Piano lessons for me started at the age of five. My teacher was a woman who lived about a mile away. She taught many of the children in and around the town, not only piano, but voice lessons as well. Several of her students were quite talented and each year under her direction, they would bring home an assortment of medals from the Peel Music Festival.

After I had been taking lessons for a couple of years, it was decided, I'm not sure by whom, that I was ready to be entered in the festival. I wasn't a naturally gifted musician by any means and I wasn't someone who spent hours practicing, but I was self-disciplined for my age and I did what was required to prepare. Oh yes, and did I mention that at that age I was loaded with self-confidence?

By the time the music festival was approaching, I had been attending grade school for a couple of years and my level of self-confidence was increasing accordingly, based on both some academic success and achievements in some athletic activities. At that age, maybe at any age now that I think about it, self-confidence can be a very fragile thing. So, success in a few areas for me personally translated into a confidence (unwarranted) in my abilities to succeed in others.

I kept telling my parents that I was going to win the gold medal at the music festival. My parents really had no way to gauge my piano skills. They had no one to compare me to and I guess they wondered if I was as good as I thought I was. I wasn't one to pound my chest and tell the world how great I was, but I had no qualms about repeatedly telling my parents that I was going to win.

My music teacher thought that perhaps she should tell my parents the *real* story of my limited piano skills. I guess my mother broached the subject when picking me up after one of my lessons. She told the teacher that I was insisting that I was going to win the piano competition and she wondered if this was possible. My music teacher's response was simple and straightforward, "He's definitely not gold medal material!"

A few weeks later, the day of the festival arrived. The audience wasn't large by any means, but I'd never played the piano for anyone other than my teacher, my parents and maybe a few other extended family members when they came to visit.

Naturally, I was a little nervous, but I guess I was able to hide it well as I strode on stage. I bowed to the audience as I had been taught and sat down at the piano. I performed my piece, got up and bowed again to polite applause. I'm not sure if I was really supposed to bow twice, but hey, the audience was clapping so why not?

Not long after that, when all of the other competitors in my age category had completed their performances, I was called on stage again, this time to receive the gold medal!

I never knew my music teacher had made that comment until years later when I was an adult and my mother told me. In the music teacher's defense, she was just trying to be honest with my parents.

Self-confidence can and does play a prominent role in many of the successes we have in life. I guess I didn't realize it at the time, but this was my example.

A Letter to Mr. Ballard

When I was in elementary school, I became a letter writer. It wasn't that I was writing them all the time, but I probably did write more than other kids my age.

There was a renowned comedian at the time named Red Skelton who had a weekly television show. I thought that he was hilarious and wouldn't it be great to do something like that when I grew up? I told my mother that I'd like to eventually replace Red Skelton when I was older. She told me I should write a letter to him and tell him just that. I didn't follow through on that, but I did start to write to some celebrities.

Most of my letters were sports related. They were sent to hockey players, usually a Toronto Maple Leaf (my favorite team). I would write a note to a specific player and tell him, in fact I'd tell each and every player I wrote to, that they were one of my favorite athletes. Of course, I would then request an autographed picture of them.

A few weeks later a photo signed by the player would arrive in the mail. I would dutifully paste it in my scrapbook and admire my growing collection.

When I got to secondary school however, the nature of my letter writing changed. Now I thought I knew as much or more about how to coach or manage a professional team than those who were actually in control. I would write, providing advice. The teenage sports fan, supplying direction to the coaches, managers and owners.

It was the early 1970's and the upstart World Hockey Association was about to begin signing players away from the NHL and begin a rival league of its own. There were many rumors floating around about which players were going to accept offers from the new league. Several of those rumors involved members of my beloved Toronto Maple Leafs of the time, a team that was improving and looked like it was ready to turn a corner with some of the good, young players they had.

The strongest rumor involved the Maple Leaf goaltender at the time, Bernie Parent. Toronto had acquired him from Philadelphia and it looked like he might become one of the best. As it turns out, a few years later he ended up back in Philadelphia and led them to two Stanley Cups. For now though, he was a Toronto Maple Leaf and certainly if the Leaf's lost him to the WHA, it would be a severe setback to their rebuilding process.

I decided to write a letter to try to encourage the team to stop Bernie from leaving. There was only one person to write to if you wanted to make a point with the Toronto Maple Leafs. It was the owner, Harold Ballard. He may have had others in the coach and manager roles, but Harold was one of those intrusive owners who made all the important decisions and everybody knew it. So, I got out my pen and paper and carefully drafted my letter.

I told Mr. Ballard that I was one of many loyal Leaf supporters who could see the team was on the upswing. I also told him that the key to victory started in goal. The Leafs had a long history of great goaltenders and the young Bernie Parent was destined to be the next one! I pleaded with the Leaf owner to "pay whatever it takes to keep Bernie Parent in a Leaf uniform. Don't let him sign with the WHA."

A couple of weeks after I mailed the letter, I opened our mailbox to find a thick envelope addressed to me with the Toronto Maple Leaf return address embossed in the upper left corner.

What could be inside? Based on its size, this had to be more than just a simple one-page reply. It looked like it could even contain season tickets!

I carefully opened the envelope and inside was a hand written letter from the owner and president of the Toronto Maple Leafs, Harold Ballard. He thanked me for my letter and added the usual company line about them always trying to improve the team. Although, I hadn't indicated my age in my letter to him, I'm sure he would have realized that I was relatively young, if for no other reason than the poor quality of my handwriting. So, in order to appease a young fan no doubt, Ballard went on to say that he was enclosing a set of team pictures that he thought I would like!

What A Concidence!

I had expected at best to get a form letter response from the hockey team. The fact that Mr. Ballard himself had taken the time to hand write his response really impressed me.

I began to flip through the player photos that he had sent me. What? It couldn't be! I flipped through them again just to be sure. Harold Ballard had sent me an autographed picture of every player on the Toronto Maple Leaf Team …. except for Bernie Parent!

Harold had dropped his hint. Bernie was as good as gone.

Bernie Parent signed a contract with the WHA that summer.

Roller Coaster or Merry-Go-Round?

We were walking back from dinner at the dining hall to our university dorm. Bill was telling us that a friend of his had this theory that everyone at various stages in their life was either on the roller coaster or the merry-go-round. Maybe it wasn't a new theory, but it was the first time I had heard it.

People were either experiencing a series of ups and downs, highs and lows in their lives or they were stuck going in circles.

They were either experiencing a range of emotions such as anticipation, fear, excitement, exhilaration, depression and disappointment OR they were stuck in a boring, predictable routine.

Sometimes, they were on one ride for a long, long time and at other times they moved freely back and forth between the two. Sometimes, they could choose which ride they were on and other times the choice seemed to be made for them. Being stuck on one or the other for a long time was probably not an ideal way to live your life.

I think everyone should try both rides and decide which they like the most. Then, try to do the things in life that allow you to stay on that favorite one whenever you can.

P.S. – If you want to try the haunted house or the magic carpet ride, that's okay too.

The Multi-purpose Essay

Some students spend their post-secondary education totally immersing themselves in that period of their life. They take full advantage of the entire educational experience. It's a time of maximum effort, exposure to new ideas and self-discovery. Others, try to get by on as little effort as possible.

It wasn't Bill this time, but it was another university acquaintance. I can't remember what his field of study was, but whatever it was, it required essay writing.

He was very, very proud of one particular essay he wrote. It didn't get published or anything like that. I'm not even sure he got a good grade on it. The reason he liked it so much was not at all related to the quality of the final product or the mark he received. It was something better than that. It was its *versatility*.

He bragged about the fact that he was able to submit this one piece of work for three different courses! Only minor adjustments were required each time to tailor it to the latest course requirement. He only wrote one essay and got credit for three! Minimum effort was a key to what he considered to be university *success*.

I Deserve an Extra Mark

It was a 12th grade English class. It was before the electronic, digital age we now live in. The students were all anxiously awaiting the return of their midterm exams. These were hard copy exams which contained long form, hand-written responses to the questions. The teacher had them piled on his desk and one by one he called out student names, each of whom came up in turn and got their exam paper returned to them.

Every student took some time to look through their own paper and examine the grade they had received. As usual there were a number of students who disagreed with the way in which their paper had been marked on some of the questions.

Unlike mathematics, where you are either right or wrong, English is a subject which can be marked subjectively. Some teachers might be inclined to value certain styles and approaches more than others. If a persuasive argument could be made, the teacher might be convinced to change the grade.

One by one, students approached the teacher, highlighted their answer to a specific question, and explained why they thought they deserved a higher mark. The teacher would review it with them individually and decide if a change was warranted.

When this process, which tended to happen every time a test or exam was returned was finally complete, the teacher looked up at the class and said, "Now, did anyone get too many marks?"

The room was silent. Nobody stepped forward to say they had received too many marks.

This was not a class that I was in. It was a story that my English teacher at the time told us about another class he had taught in a prior year. He told us the story while he was in the middle of returning our papers. He ended his story by telling us that he had given every single student in that class an extra mark that they did not deserve. While many had approached him to argue for more marks, nobody had indicated they had received too many. I guess there's a little bit of a cheat in all of us!

P.S. – I think he extended his experiment to our class because he gave me nine marks on a question that was only worth eight. I didn't tell him.

Dear Mr. Bassett

As I got older, my letter writing became bolder.

I moved on from requesting autographed pictures of my favorite athletes to providing suggestions/advice to sports coaches, managers and administrators. Now I figured I was ready to apply for a job. The word *ready* is actually a bit of a stretch, but what the heck, I had nothing to lose.

I was 17 years old and the Toronto Argonauts Football Club of the CFL had fired Leo Cahill and were looking for a new head coach. I decided to apply.

The letter this time went to John Bassett, Chairman & President of Baton Broadcasting, and owner of the Toronto Argonauts. It described my own limited experience playing for my high school football team. Oh yes and I also played for a local flag football team. It went on to say that playing ability did not necessarily translate into coaching ability and there were many examples of successful coaches who hadn't played at a high level themselves.

The advantages to hiring a teenager to coach the team? I promised my salary would not be too high. Fan interest would be stimulated and crowds would likely increase, coming to the games to see this first in professional sports. I showed my *maturity* by talking about the importance of open and honest communication amongst all members of the organization and I directly referred to a negative incident that had occurred between two players the previous season. I also explained that while I would oversee everything, assistant coaches would play more prominent roles. I would just be a figurehead.

I ended my letter with a quote. I doubt Mr. Bassett would recognize it, unless he also read the fictional Chip Hilton series of sports books as a youngster. "Repetition is the secret of all knowledge."

This was the first job I had actually applied for by writing a formal letter. Summer jobs had just been a matter of filling out an application or talking to someone you knew in those days. But, would I get a reply?

Fast Forward 3 weeks

Surprisingly, yes!

I got a business-like reply from Mr. Bassett. Not unexpectedly however, I didn't get the job. I didn't even get an interview.

My rejection letter from John Bassett follows. Focus on the positive. He "admired my nerve."

What A Concidence!

Letter from former Toronto Argonaut President John Bassett

101 RICHMOND STREET WEST, SUITE 1206
TORONTO 110, ONTARIO 364-6491

OFFICE OF THE CHAIRMAN AND PRESIDENT

November 27, 1972.

Mr. Larry Proctor,
Box 42,
Caledon East, Ontario.

Dear Larry:

        In answer to your letter of November 22nd, while I admire your nerve, I am sure you recognize that you do not have the qualifications to be a coach of a professional football team.

        I do, however, advise you to keep on with your interest in football and perhaps at some later date you may fulfil your ambition.

        Yours sincerely,

JB/jc   John Bassett.

The Summer Job Interview

I was a university student looking for a summer job. The company my father worked for hired students as security guards to cover for the full-timers when they were on vacation. I was one of several being considered this time around and most of the candidates had a parent who had a permanent job in one of the many departments there.

The Manager of Security conducted the interview. He asked if I had any previous security experience of any kind. My answer was an honest one, "No, I don't."

Do you have any fire prevention experience? "No."

Do you have any first aid training? "No."

Have you ever taken any health and safety training? "No, I'm sorry I haven't."

"Well, your Dad is a pretty good guy, so you're hired."

NEPOTISM - For a definition, see the story above.

The New Career Interview

I'd spent 15 years at an aircraft manufacturing company. It's an industry that's very cyclical in nature with lots of ups and downs.

I'd survived some previous layoffs, but this one was larger. It was also a different type of downsizing. Instead of having to say goodbye to people because the company didn't have enough orders to employ the current workforce, this time a decision was made to permanently stop building one specific model of airplane. This particular aircraft wasn't seen as being relevant anymore and not likely to be profitable going forward. A lot of the people being laid off this time would probably never be recalled.

As part of the layoff process, there was an outplacement service provided. Job search workshops, needs assessments and career exploration classes were offered. The organization hired to do this suddenly had a need for another counsellor to help facilitate the classes, not just for our company, but for many other manufacturing organizations that were going through layoffs as well. The decision was made to let some of the employees affected by the reduction in staff to apply for the role. I was one of those who applied.

Even though I had primarily been working in finance related roles and had taken many business courses, my degree was actually in Social Psychology. This facilitator position would be totally different from what I was used to doing, but sometimes you have to reinvent yourself. It was becoming more and more common that individuals not only worked for several different companies in their lifetime, but also eventually had several different careers as well.

On the day of the interview, I waited patiently in the reception area. I had only worked for one company since finishing university, so naturally I was a little nervous. I had been through some internal interviews at the manufacturing company, but this was the first time with an external organization.

There were a few others who had applied, including Diana. She had worked in the same department as me and had also been laid off. As it turned out, her interview was scheduled immediately prior to mine.

A lot of organizations would not allow this to happen, but the logistics of this workplace were such that those who had completed their interview, left the building via the same reception area where others were still awaiting their turn.

Diana saw me sitting there and immediately came over to say hello. She went on to say, "Larry, this job is not for me, but it would be perfect for you!" She also began to tell me what many of the questions were that she had been asked in the interview. Suddenly, I felt a lot more prepared!

Approximately five to ten minutes later, I was called into the interview room. A funny thing about interviews, it's often difficult to know how

What A Concidence!

you've done. Some interviewers seem more positive than others and make all of the candidates think they've done well. Others don't smile much and leave you wondering what you should or shouldn't have said.

I wouldn't say I aced it, but I did get the feeling I had done reasonably well. On the way home I stopped off to get a few things at the mall. By the time I did get home, there was a message for me to call the manager who had interviewed me. I called back immediately. I got the job!

Thanks Diana! It sure helps when you know the questions in advance.

Fast Forward 20 Years

Jeremy, our son, having recently graduated from university, is sitting in the reception area of a small office awaiting his first fulltime job interview. The acoustics are such that he can hear another candidate being interviewed in a room nearby. Jeremy can hear both the questions and the answers. Similar to his dad twenty years earlier, he has a head start when his own interview begins. He also got the job!

Welcome to Nassau

We had been in Nassau for two days and were sitting in the lobby of our hotel. Harald and I made the trip together. Two single, mid-twenties guys who were friends since high school football days. He was the quarterback and I was the wide receiver.

Harald noticed a new group of arriving vacationers about to disembark from their airport shuttle bus. He leaped to his feet and positioned himself so they would have to pass by him as they entered the hotel. "Welcome to Nassau", he said as he smiled and shook their hands. They assumed he was part of the official hotel welcoming committee. No, he was just Harald, and in his own way he had made many new friends.

That was Harald, the outgoing, always positive, real estate agent friend, demonstrating how easy it was for him to meet people. I guess you have to have that type of personality to survive in his business. To illustrate how positive he could be, I think back to the morning after we arrived in the Bahamas. Harald jumped out of bed, pulled open the curtains and started exclaiming "what a beautiful day it is!" This was despite the fact it was overcast and drizzling rain!

I'm not exactly a world traveler, but I've been on a few vacations and I have never met as many people as I did when I travelled with Harald to Nassau.

Harald could strike up a conversation with anyone. On the plane ride home, we decided to see how many names of people we had met in one week that we could remember. The number was around fifty. There were others who we also talked to and partied with, but we just couldn't remember their names. I guess if you stand in the lobby welcoming people to Nassau as if you have lived there all your life, you're bound to meet a lot of people.

The other thing about Harald, the real estate agent, was that he wasn't afraid of rejection. He once told me that he could knock on 100 doors and get the door slammed in his face 99 times, but if he got the listing at the hundredth door, it was all worthwhile. I think I'd go back home after the second or third door closed on me.

Now, I obviously wouldn't have met nearly as many people if I hadn't been travelling with Harald. That could have easily been the case. When we first arrived in Nassau, I was worried I might be spending the week alone.

At the time, all I required to enter the country was my birth certificate or driver's license. I didn't need a passport. Harald was not a Canadian citizen, having been born in Germany and emigrating to Canada as an infant, so he needed a passport.

He did bring a passport, the same one he used to enter Canada over 20 years before with the official photo being his baby picture! The Bahamian customs official was not impressed, but after some stern warnings allowed him to stay and we had our mid-winter break in the sun.

Fast Forward 20 Years

Harald and his wife returned to Nassau for a vacation of their own. Harald was a real fitness buff and the morning after they arrived, he woke early and left a note for his wife that he had gone for a run and would meet her at breakfast.

He never returned. They found his body a day later, a drowning victim. Although details were sketchy, it appeared he had probably slipped near some rocks, banged his head, knocking himself unconscious and fallen into the sea.

He made many friends throughout his life and we were all shocked to learn of this tragedy.

At Harald's funeral, I was of course reminded of our own trip to Nassau. Harald seemed to have endless energy throughout the day, moving from one activity to the next. When he finally did decide to call it a day though, sleep would come quickly for him. He was a deep sleeper and a loud snorer.

I always knew I had to try to get to sleep before him, because if I didn't, he would start to snore and I'd never get to sleep! Usually though,

Harald would be the first to drift off and I would be lying there listening to the ever-increasing volume of his snoring.

One time I even resorted to throwing my sneaker at him to try and wake him when his snoring was just too much to take. The hope was, that for that brief time that he awoke before he fell back into his deep sleep, I might be able to get to sleep too.

Many stories were told at his funeral. I only wished on that day I could have thrown a shoe at him to wake him. That could not be done of course, but I could vividly picture what he'd be doing. He'd be standing and smiling at everyone, with a hand extended saying, "Welcome to Heaven!"

Toilet Training

We had started to toilet train Jeremy and were stressing the importance of the associated good hygiene habits. Always wash your hands thoroughly with soap and water after going to the washroom.

Things were progressing well and one day he said he had to go pee. I took him to the washroom and he pulled down his pants and stood in front of the toilet. Just before he started, he turned to me and said, "You hold **it** Dad**,** so I won't have to wash my hands when I'm done".

My Sister, the Boy

One day, when my sister was a toddler, she asked my parents when she would *turn into a boy*. She thought that this was something that eventually happened to everyone.

Since I was two years older, she assumed it had already happened to me and her time was coming soon. My friends were all boys and were around my age. Her friends were all girls and were around her age. So, there was no real confusion in her mind. The transformation was going to happen. It was just a matter of time.

When it was my turn to speak at my sister's wedding, I related the story to the invited guests. "As a child, Diane thought she would eventually turn into a boy", I said. I went on to tell her new husband that it hadn't happened yet, but he needed to be aware, just in case it happened that night!

The marriage didn't last, but I don't think that was the reason.

P.S. - Another thing about my sister. My mother tells us that when she was out walking with the two of us as toddlers and we were about to cross a street, she would reach out to hold our hands before crossing. I would gladly take her hand, but my sister would not. She would pull her hand away and refuse. She had an independent streak, even at a very young age. As we got older, she wound up being the much more extroverted of the two of us. Some traits seem definitely to be inborn.

Tomorrow's Leaders

I attended Victoria College at the University of Toronto. Former Prime Minister Lester B. Pearson did too. Award winning movie director Norman Jewison was another famous VIC grad. In fact, there were a number of alumni who went on to prominence in their chosen fields, as might be said for many other colleges and universities throughout the country.

While a student there, I certainly didn't look at those around me and try to project for them any specific future distinction, status or celebrity. We all just seemed like typical young adults, getting an education that would prove to be a valuable asset somewhere down the road.

In some ways though, you might expect there to be at least a modest level of intellect and maturity. In fact, there was a significantly wide range of both.

Each year the men's residence would have a special Christmas dinner in Burwash Hall. If you are a little bit younger and are not familiar with Victoria College or Burwash Hall in particular, think Harry Potter.

The regular staff would prepare the meal, but the place would be decorated in a festive way and the meal itself would of course be turkey and all the trimmings. Wine was served and each place at the immaculately polished, long, wooden tables had an apple with a small candle in it. When lit, the candles all in a row gave the room a magical Christmas glow.

Everyone was expected to dress in a suit and tie for this particular meal and to any outsider peeking in, they would see an impressive group of young gentlemen. Guys only. The residences were segregated back then.

Approaching the end of a term was reason enough for students to celebrate and some overdid it. That overindulgence in some cases meant the consumption, make that the overconsumption, of alcohol. Much more than the one glass of wine served with dinner was drunk by many of those in attendance. That may help explain what happened next.

Students sat at tables designated for their own specific *house* or residence, around twenty-five for each. Sometimes there were rivalries between houses that carried over from the sports fields or whatever other competitive situation might exist.

Who knows how it started, but at some point someone from one table threw something at someone sitting at another. The inevitable retaliation occurred and suddenly a fully-fledged food fight began. This was **before** the 1978 movie Animal House and its famous food fight scene. Not everyone participated in the Burwash Hall version, but anyone in the dining hall couldn't escape the fact that they were in the middle of it.

Food of every description was thrown, right down to the mashed potatoes. The student sitting beside me was about to take a sip of wine from his glass when an apple came whizzing by, knocking and breaking the glass right out of his hand. Many dishes were broken. Clothes were stained. The university leaders were appalled.

One of my friends at the time said, "It's hard to believe that here in this room, are many of the business, political and academic leaders of tomorrow."

Tracking Down the Culprit

When Jeremy returned later that night, he came in the door with news he knew we wouldn't like. He had driven the car to his soccer practice. He was seventeen and hadn't had his license too long at the time.

The car had damage to the front fender, bumper and headlight. He didn't know who did it or how it happened because he was on the soccer field when it occurred.

The soccer parking lot wasn't nearly large enough for the number of cars that used it on a typical summer evening. This was especially true when people arrived for the late games which started around 8:00 or 8:30 at night. They had to find spots before the families with younger children, whose games started at 6:30 or 7:00, had left and opened up some parking spaces.

So, Jeremy like many others, had found a spot to park on the side of the road. One of those drivers that left before he did, must have dinged our car as they drove away from the soccer fields, because there weren't any other vehicles near it when Jeremy went to leave and discovered the damage.

There were two pieces of information that had been left on the windshield under the wiper. One was a small corner of a piece of paper with the words "Call me about your car", followed by a telephone number. The other was a business card, with a note that said, "I saw who hit your car. Call if there is a problem."

I tried calling the number on the first note that presumably had been left by whoever accidently damaged our vehicle. There was no answer and no voice mail. Oh well I thought, perhaps it's a business with no answering service or if it's a residence, they aren't home. I'll try again tomorrow during the day.

When I called the number the next day, I did get an answer. It was a business alright, but the person who answered didn't know anything about damage to a car. He said he would ask around the office, but it was a private business line and he was pretty sure no one there had been involved.

I quickly began to realize what had happened. Whoever had hit our car recognized that there were witnesses, so they had written a note and left it on the windshield to make it appear as though they were being a responsible citizen, but the telephone number they left was simply one they had made up.

I moved on to the contact number on the business card that had been left on the windshield. This fellow had indeed witnessed the incident. He told me the make, model and color of the SUV that had hit our car and a license plate number that he was sure was close, although he couldn't say for sure it was 100% accurate.

So now we had a little more information, but no way of using it to find the name and address of the person responsible. This is where my wife, Margaret, took over. She noticed that the scrap of paper the first note was written on, was in fact the back of a receipt or invoice of some sort and there was a signature scrawled on the other side. The note writer had apparently hastily torn a piece from a document that they had in their car.

We tried to decipher the name. It started with an "H" but it wasn't totally legible. After studying it for a while we came to the conclusion that the surname was "Hollman". For the purposes of this story, the name has been changed to protect the guilty.

Now we moved on to the telephone listings and the internet. This is where we encountered a bit of luck. We assumed the guilty party lived nearby in Bolton, since the damage occurred at the local soccer field. Margaret discovered there was only one "Hollman" with a telephone listing in this particular town, so we copied down the address and phone number.

Another little coincidence which proved to be very helpful; a friend of our daughter's lived on the same street as the Hollmans! Margaret made a quick call to her and told her the house number.

"Is this house close to yours?"

Almost directly across the street as it turned out.

"Would you mind going outside and casually checking the type of vehicle in their driveway?"

What A Concidence!

The SUV she described matched the make, model and color of the one our witness had provided. The license plate number she quoted matched with the exception of one digit.

Hmmm, I had another call to make. I think I'll just pretend that the note this person left on our car had their correct phone number on it.

I dialed the number we had wanted all along and asked, "Is this the Hollmans?"

"Yes", a male voice replied.

"I'm just calling about the damage that happened to my car at the soccer field on Tuesday night. You left a note on my windshield." I didn't mention the phony telephone number.

CLICK. He hung up on me!

I waited a few minutes and dialed again. This time after about five rings I got an answering machine.

The message I left went something like this. "Your name is Hollman. Your address is… You accidently hit my vehicle at the soccer field. A witness provided me with a description of your vehicle and the license plate number. Call me back in ten minutes or I'll have to report this to the police."

Less than five minutes later our phone rang. The culprit apologized and confessed. He went on to say he had become flustered at the time because his wife was pregnant.

"I'm not the father, so don't take it out on me!", I said. Well, I didn't actually say that. I just thought it.

He told me that if I got an estimate, he would pay to repair the damage.

Fast Forward 2 Weeks

The car was repaired and we received a cheque to cover the cost. I'm sure he must have been puzzled as to how we tracked him down. He probably thought we had a police officer friend or someone else who had access to a database of license plate numbers. The fact is the key piece of evidence was his own signature on the back of a piece of paper that he himself had left on our windshield!

Revenge on the Noisy Neighbors

Brian was my neighbor. He and his family were good neighbors. I think they'd say the same about us.

Brian travelled a lot for his job. Most of that travel would be through the week. One particular weeknight, he was hoping to get to sleep early because he had an early morning flight the next day.

Another of Brian's neighbors, for whatever reason, was having a party that night, a loud party. It was a warm summer night, so their windows were open and the music was booming. It kept playing. The party went on into the wee hours of the morning. Brian hadn't had a wink of sleep and his alarm was set to go off in a couple of hours.

Needless to say, he wasn't in the best of moods when he got up early to leave for the airport. Getting by on a couple of hours of sleep can do that to you.

Just before he left home, Brian went into his garage and got his lawn mower out. He checked to make sure it had lots of gas. It would probably run for at least an hour on a full tank. He pushed the mower to the back of his yard and parked it right beside the fence that separated his property from his partying neighbors of the night before. He pulled the cord and was pleased it started on the first pull. It seemed to be running well too.

With not much other activity or noise in the neighborhood so early in the morning, the lawn mower sounded even louder than normal. Brian was pleased.

He hopped into his car and headed for the airport. After all, he had a flight to catch.

A Daughter's Love at a Convenient Time

Laura was quite young at the time, so I decided to ride with her down one of those magic carpet rides at an amusement park. We were at the top of the slide, which I'm sure seemed pretty high and scary to her. She was sitting in front of me on the carpet. Just before we pushed off, she turned around to me and said, "Dad, I love you."

A Son's Love at a Convenient Time

Jeremy, a toddler at the time, and Margaret, his mom, were in the bathroom. Jeremy was sitting on the toilet when he began to tell his mom how beautiful she was and how much he loved her. "To the moon and back, to the sun and back, to the end of the universe and back", he said. Wow, his mom was impressed and flattered and proud.

Just the type of comment from a 4-year-old that can bring a tear to a mother's eye. Then he said, "Mom, can you wipe my bum?"

Career Ambitions

Doctor, lawyer, firefighter, pro athlete, what did your kids want to be when they grew up? How about a cement maker?

Laura was 6 years old. She was playing tee ball, so of course when it came time to purchase pictures, we thought we'd like to get one of the trading cards. You know, the kind that kids (and adults at times) collect. Normally it's professional players with their picture on the front and some personal information and statistics on the back.

The back of Laura's card contained the usual stats as well as her career ambitions.

Laura wanted to be either a Spice Girl (they were the popular pre-teen group at the time) or a cement maker (absolutely no idea where that came from).

Somewhere along the way, her career path took her away from cement making to teaching. I guess there were no post-grad degrees in cement making.

Café de Soir

The Café de Soir was established sometime in the mid 1970's. It was described as a newly opened, small restaurant that featured light French cuisine at reasonable prices. The ad appeared in the university newspaper, so it was to be assumed that the café would appeal to the young adults who read that publication. A telephone number was provided because reservations were recommended.

The two fellows who established the Café de Soir lived in the same university student residence as I did. Let's refer to them as Don and Blair. The phone number provided was theirs. The idea of the restaurant had existed somewhere in their imaginations.

If they were going to pull this off, they would have to stay in character. Initially they had to keep reminding themselves when answering their phone to make sure they said "Hello, Café de Soir", rather than just their normal hello.

Before you knew it, they had started to take reservations for their new business venture. They would note the customer's name, as well as the date and time they would like to dine, on a note pad next to their phone.

As the day of their first reservation quickly approached, Don and Blair could hardly contain their excitement.

There wasn't much preparation required though, no cleaning or decorating to do. No menus to prepare. No waiters or waitresses to train. As a matter of fact, they didn't even have a chef! Actually, the address of this imaginary café that appeared in the newspaper ad didn't even exist!

The street name was real. However, the street number didn't exist. Numbers lower and higher could be found, but where one would expect the café to be, there was nothing.

The confused prospective patrons showed up at their scheduled time. They then tended to pace back and forth where they thought the café should be. They might even pull a note from their pocket to double check the address of their dining destination.

If any of them had decided to look up at one of the college residence room windows that overlooked the sidewalk, they would have seen Don and Blair laughing hysterically.

The Café de Soir wasn't around very long. How could it be? It never really existed! No further ads were placed and neither Don nor Blair ended up working in the hospitality industry.

P.S. – These two were also known for their *School of Hard Knocks*. This was what happened when someone politely knocked on their door, only to have Don or Blair slam a hockey stick against the inside of that door, resulting in what sounded like a small bomb exploding. The unsuspecting visitor would have the crap scared out of them.

Con Job

I can't remember his name, but I can remember his story.

He didn't offer anything more than the basics about himself initially and when he finally did open up, he didn't provide all of the details.

I was a co-facilitator for a government funded Career Exploration program. The participants were all unemployed and unable to return to the type of job they had held. There were many reasons why returning to the work they had done previously was no longer possible; the changing economy, different skill sets now required, or companies closing and moving elsewhere as the global economy began to take root.

Our job was to help these people through a series of self-analysis exercises. We would assist them in identifying their transferable skills, their strengths and interests, and then through an exploration process, help them consider possible new career directions. This all happened over a 6-week period.

None of the participants knew each other. Everyone would introduce themselves on the first day, but generally be reluctant to reveal too much about who they were. It was amazing how this would inevitably change over the course of the program. A real camaraderie would develop. The bonding would continue, so that when it came to the final day when everyone would say their goodbyes, it could be quite emotional. Not everyone would have jobs by then, but all would now have some direction and support.

During Week #4, we were doing a workshop that allowed the participants to tell everyone a little bit more about themselves.

That's when it happened. One group member, who to that point had been nothing more than that, a nondescript member of the group, stood up and began to tell us his story. He had recently been released from prison.

He hoped to begin a new life. He never told us exactly what his crime was, other than to say he "did some very bad things", bad enough that he spent a few years behind bars. He did his time in British Columbia and was now in Ontario looking for a new start.

We all looked at him a little differently from that point on. I'm sure that there were some who feared him, everyone was definitely a little more wary, but there was also a hope that he would find a way to a reputable job and some future success.

When we moved on to the job search part of the program, we helped him with his resume which listed a cooking program he had taken at Matsqui Institute. Matsqui is a medium security prison in Abbotsford, BC. He was looking for employment as a sous chef now and it was important that this education be included on his resume.

Not only did we help workshop participants with their resumes, we also helped with their job search and interview skills. During a taped mock job interview we did with this particular participant, we perused his resume as a prospective employer would and then mentioned that we hadn't heard of this "Matsqui Institute". Afterall, the interviewee might well be questioned on this.

He probably hoped that if he was asked a question like this, that it would be much better if the interviewer did not know anything about "Matsqui". So how would he respond? He simply said it was a small facility in British Columbia, which of course it was! He managed to answer all of our questions and sell himself during those practice sessions, without ever being dishonest.

We talked about the importance of networking and he demonstrated some ingenuity with that too in his personal job search. He had a friend who delivered bread to local restaurants, so one day he rode along with him and at every stop he got out of the delivery van, spoke to the owner, manager, chef or whoever the potential decision maker might be. A resume would be left, a number to call and he hoped that through one of these leads, he would eventually land a job.

In a way, despite this man's criminal past, he became the unofficial star of the workshop. He recognized his situation, took advice readily and worked hard to get a job. He supported the group and they supported him.

Fast Forward Zero Weeks

Before this particular Career Exploration program ended, the man with the mysterious background had found a job. In fact, he was the first person from the group to become employed. There is no coincidence here, just a human being using his talents and resourcefulness, stressing the positives along the way and it ultimately resulting in a personal success story.

Little Things (about me) that Bug my Wife

I'm sure there are bigger and more irritating things about me that bother my wife, but here are some of the smaller ones:

When the label on the back of my sweatshirt is sticking up and out.

How hard I bang on the keyboard when typing.

How long I keep my clothes and how many of them don't really fit properly.

When I buy single ply toilet paper and the roll is gone in no time.

The force and noise I make when I shift sleeping positions in bed at night.

What a noisy eater I am

That's enough for now.

Of course, in keeping with sound marital advice, I can't think of one thing about my wife that ever irritates me in any way.

New Words

My wife makes up words and expressions. Among them, "schmaltzy", which during a game of scrabble she later proved is a real word, meaning "things that are extremely sentimental." (She doesn't like movies, or stories, or songs that are too schmaltzy).

Other examples include "humma, humma, ding-dong". This is apparently an expression that can be used in place of a sigh.

Then there's "Huey, Dewy & Louie", as in "Huey, Dewey & Louie, it's hot out there!" or conversely, "Huey, Dewy & Louie, it's cold in here!"

The "N" Word

My grandmother, my mom's mom, was a hard-working lady throughout her entire life and she lived well into her nineties. She passed away before the turn of the twenty first century.

She raised seven children on a farm in rural Ontario. Her chores went well beyond the child rearing and those of the household itself. She did much of the farm work too, especially after my grandfather decided to start a trucking business and was on the road a lot.

Grandma was someone whose work was never done, a woman who thought of others before herself and who was active in her church and her community.

At one point, when she was in her eighties, she spent some time in the hospital. While there, she would strike up a conversation with whoever else might be around.

The nurse who was assigned to her room was one of those who talked with my grandmother and they both asked each other questions about their backgrounds and their families.

Grandma proceeded to tell the nurse about her seven children, four girls and three boys growing up on the farm. They were all well grounded and had daily chores to complete she said. As a matter of fact, "they worked like n-----s!"

My grandmother had lived all her life in rural Ontario; white, rural Ontario, where an expression like the one she used, sadly, was not uncommon. In fact, in her eyes it was a compliment. She saw it as a phrase that demonstrated how hard her kids had worked growing up and equated that with a hard-working, black person.

However, her nurse, who incidentally was black, did not see it that way. She was quite offended by the statement and rightly so.

That nurse was never assigned to my grandmother's room again after that day. Grandma deeply regretted what she had said. She was a God-fearing lady who because of one innocently uttered statement, created an image of herself in someone else's mind, that was as far from the truth of who she really was as one could imagine.

The Senior's Shopping List

My uncle Jim, actually he was my Dad's uncle, so he was my great uncle, lived next door. He was a widower and a retired school teacher. Teaching methods of his day (1930s-1950s) were quite different than they are today. He often said, "If I can't drive the message in through the eyes and ears, I'll send it up the arm!" The tool he used to send it up the arm was the strap.

I'm not sure whether it would have been his nature anyway, or if it was as a result of being a teacher for so many years, but after he retired and his wife died, he planned his life meticulously. He lived on a schedule. He had a routine that he followed weekly and didn't really like it when it was disrupted.

Once when he was out for dinner with a large group, the waiter came round to take their orders. Before anyone else could speak, Uncle Jim said, "We'll all have fish and chips." He had ordered for the whole table without giving anyone else a chance to even open their mouth!

It wasn't as though he had offered to pay for the group and wanted to limit the size of the bill. No one was quite sure why he did it. Maybe he just wanted to speed up the process.

At home, he ate the same meals on the same days each and every week. As such, his shopping list was always the same too. One regular item on the list every week was eggs, not a dozen eggs though, only nine. That's right, he bought nine eggs each week. He had one for breakfast each day and two days a week he had another for lunch.

The local shopkeepers knew him, were used to his order, and gave him want he wanted.

Are we all destined to be this set in our ways as we enter our golden years?

I've never tried to buy nine eggs at a supermarket. I wonder what the response would be.

The Roommate

Joe was in his second year at the University of Guelph. Residence spots were almost exclusively for first year students.

Together, Joe and a couple of his friends found a suitable house near campus that they could rent for the upcoming school term. The house had four bedrooms. They decided to take it, but to make it work financially they would have to find someone else to join the three of them in renting the place.

They placed an ad in the university newspaper and posted flyers around the area.

It wasn't long before they got a telephone call from an interested party. The prospective roommate agreed to meet them the next day and check out the room. When the time came however, he didn't show up for his appointment. There was no call to explain why he didn't make it.

A few days went by, the extra room was still vacant and the phone rang again. It was the same guy who had called previously. He said he was still interested in the room and would like to schedule another time to come and see it.

Well guess what? That time came and went too, and again he was a no show, and again no call of explanation as to why he had not come to see the room.

When he called for a third time after another few days had passed, Joe and his roommates had begun to wonder about the guy. They were surprised this time when he said he would take the room, sight unseen. He just wanted to know if he could move in soon. Joe and his buddies, by this time desperate for someone to share the costs with, had no objections.

New Roomie moved in a couple of days later. He showed up in his leather university jacket, but with few other personal belongings. He was taller than average, muscular and didn't smile much. He didn't seem to have any textbooks, wasn't very talkative and no one was quite sure what program he was enrolled in.

As time went by, Joe and his friends began to notice some strange things about their new roommate. He certainly didn't come across as a typical college student. There were very few conversations between him and any of the other three.

There were some disturbing signs though. Some of their food was starting to disappear. While Joe and his three friends shared some of their food, some was definitely meant to be their own and they all contributed to the cost of groceries. The new roommate did not. The amount of food that disappeared increased in the days and weeks that followed.

Something else had started to happen too. New Roomie started to wear their clothes! He didn't seem to have many of his own, so he helped himself to theirs wherever there was a fit.

They now realized this fellow wasn't a student at all and he wasn't the type they wanted for a roommate. They were genuinely frightened of him. They were afraid to ask him to stop eating their food. They were afraid to ask him to stop wearing their clothes. They were afraid to even talk to him. His portion of the rent was going unpaid. They didn't want him around anymore, but were not about to ask him to leave. He was one scary guy.

The decision was made to avoid him as much as possible, try to keep to themselves and at the end of the term, they would all move out. From that point on they no longer heard from him or knew anything about him, until ……

Fast Forward 5 years

Joe and his friends are sitting in a courtroom. They're listening to the testimony of someone they once knew, a man around their age, who ultimately is convicted of the rape and brutal murder of an innocent female victim. A murder, in which the victim's body when discovered was horribly mutilated. It was a front-page story in all of the Toronto newspapers at the time.

What A Concidence!

The man guilty of the horrific crime had been in prison previously, they discovered. Now, he would be going back. In between prison terms, he had been their roommate.

P.S. – This is a tale of caution you may want to tell your children before they go off to college or university.

The Accident

It was early September, a busy time if you work at a college like I did at the time, or a school, like my wife did. It was also the day I returned to work from bereavement leave, following the death of my father-in-law.

My phone rang a little after mid-day. The caller explained that she was the owner of the local flower shop at the corner of Airport Road and Old Church Road. She knew my mother and had somehow found out where I worked.

"Your mom has been hit by a car! She's conscious, but she is in a lot of pain. An ambulance has been called and they are taking her to the hospital."

"Okay, I'll get there as soon as I can." My mind was racing as I drove to the hospital, fearing the worst, but hoping for the best.

Mom was a week away from her eighty-fifth birthday. She was walking home, having just left the salon where she had her weekly hair appointment. She waited for the light to change before beginning to cross Airport Road via the crosswalk at the intersection. When she was about half way across, a pick-up truck pulled out of the adjacent liquor store parking lot and proceeded to turn left into the crosswalk.

The truck hit my mom and knocked her to the pavement. There were quite a few witnesses, some of whom she knew. A couple of them carried her to the edge of the road. She was dazed, but coherent. She also had a lot of pain in her left side.

While the bystanders showed their concern for mom, the driver of the truck backed it up out of the intersection and into the parking lot he had just exited. He wanted to get his vehicle off the road to avoid blocking traffic, right? Yes, but he then proceeded to turn his truck around and leave the scene via the parking lot's rear exit!

Very soon after the incident, both the police and an ambulance arrived. The ambulance whisked mom away to the hospital. A concerned neighbor accompanied her. Meanwhile, the OPP put out a call to all of their local officers to be on the lookout for the hit-and-run vehicle.

Several witnesses were able to provide an accurate description of the pickup truck. Oh yes, he also had a vanity license plate. It was easy to remember too, "IM IRISH".

With this information, the police were able to arrive at his residence shortly after he did. They administered a breathalyzer test and then charged him with "Impaired Driving" and "Leaving the Scene of an Accident".

When I arrived at the hospital, they were taking mom for x-rays. The results didn't show any breaks. Hospital staff tried to get her up on her feet, but she was in too much pain to stand. Through it all she remained stoic, never shedding a tear.

They decided to do more tests and those results were quite different. She had a broken pelvis on her left side, a cracked right pelvis and several cracked ribs. Fortunately, very fortunately, she hadn't suffered any trauma to her head.

So, mom spent the next six weeks in the hospital. That's where we celebrated her 85th birthday. She then moved to another facility for a couple of weeks to continue her rehab, before eventually getting back home.

Mom was always a very determined person, and she worked hard at her rehab. She had shown similar determination after my Dad had died a few years earlier, intending to prove to everyone that she was quite capable of looking after herself on her own.

After the accident, she was never able to be as active as she had been previously though. Initially, she had to use a walker to walk, but she eventually was able to get around with just a cane. She continued to live alone and welcome the large circle of friends she had come to know over the years.

Fast Forward 18 Months

The driver of the truck with the "IM IRISH" license plate is now in court. He's been found guilty and is awaiting his sentencing. Incidentally, he also had a previous DUI charge.

He hangs his head and weeps as he's told he will be spending the next 10 months in jail.

The Glass is Not Empty

Some stories stick with you. This one came from a Sunday morning church service. It was told as a children's story, but I suspect it was meant more for the adults in the congregation.

The minister held up an empty glass and asked the children what it contained. They examined the glass closely and responded that there was nothing in it. After being told that was incorrect and that indeed there was something in the glass, one of the children gave the answer "air".

"Yes", the minister said, "there is air in the glass. Now can anyone tell me how to get the air out of the glass?"

He turned the glass upside down and said, "If I turn it upside down, will the air fall out?"

The answer was "No".

He shook the glass and asked, "Can I shake it out?"

"No" again.

Well, he explained, you could hook up a fairly sophisticated device like a vacuum and suck the air out.

However, there was an easier way to get the air out. The minister took a pitcher of water and poured it into the glass. The water had now displaced the air. The water had forced the air out of the glass.

So, what's the analogy for this story? The minister pointed to his heart and said, "When something is in here that is bothering you, you cannot shake it out or simply throw it away. You have to put something in there to replace it."

A life lesson worth remembering and one you can pass on to others when they need it. I've done so many times.

Preparation for the Real World

Did your schooling actually prepare you for the real world? Were you lucky enough to have summer or part-time jobs that were in a field that was the same, or similar to your eventual career? Maybe not, but hopefully at least some of the skills you learned were transferable.

My summer and part-time jobs were pretty wide-ranging. In no particular order, here they are and what they taught me.

Accounting Clerk – there can be some very boring tasks that are part of a daily office job.

Hockey School Counsellor – even if there are no openings, if you write a good enough letter seeking a summer job, they might create a position for you. Also, if you are young and really ambitious (this would be my boss, not me), the sky's the limit. Four years later, at the age of twenty-five, he became the youngest head coach in the history of the NHL.

Security Guard - it's really difficult to stay awake when you're on the night shift.

Recreational Hockey Referee & Baseball Umpire – there's always somebody who thinks you made the wrong call.

Beer Store Clerk – based on the number of empties they returned, some people drink a lot of beer.

Radio Sports Reporter – doing this in the evening while holding down a full-time day job, meant for some long days. However, it was rewarding to hear my recorded self on the radio as I drove to work in the morning. It also convinced me I didn't want to sacrifice a secure full-time position for the long shot chance at a more exciting career.

Spot Welder – wow, I think I went a full hour without a fully formed thought passing through my head. I couldn't do this for a living. It's very hot in the factory and mind dulling. Better stay in school and get a good education.

Cable Television Host – if you write a decent proposal, the government might give you a grant that will employ you and two other students for the summer. You will promote and publicize local sports through the production of a weekly cable television show. You will decide on the content, write the script, interview and film the athletes and help with the editing. Just don't try to do a phone-in show in case no one calls.

One Way Conversation

Have you ever had a conversation with your spouse where one of you does all of the talking and the other offers no response at all?

My brother-in-law, Joe, pulled the car in front of his parent's house and waited for them at the curb so he could drive them to church.

Usually, my father-in-law, Jaime, would sit in the front passenger seat and my mother-in-law, Albertina, would be in the back. This day was no different. Jaime got in the front seat, closed the door behind him and Albertina closed her door firmly as well. Joe drove away, heading for the church which was about ten minutes from their home.

There was a little conversation during the drive, albeit one sided on this particular Sunday. Jaime commented and questioned Albertina on a few things during the short trip.

They pulled up in front of the church where Joe stopped to let his parents out of the car. Jaime got out but Albertina didn't. They looked around and she wasn't even in the car! What happened? Where could she be?

A quick return drive to the house found her still standing on the sidewalk. Turns out after initially deciding to get in the driver's side of the back seat of the car, she changed her mind due to something on the floor of the car, closed the door and started to walk around behind the car to get in the passenger side. Joe upon hearing the door slam shut, assumed she was in the car and pulled away, heading for the church without so much as a glance to the back seat.

We asked how they could drive there and not realize she wasn't in the vehicle. Didn't Jaime think it was strange that he would be talking to his wife and she wasn't responding at all? Nah, that wasn't unusual he said.

Come to think of it, maybe a lot of husbands would say the same thing. And the wives would probably say they only respond when there's something worth responding to.

The Conditioned Response

And sometimes you respond without really listening to what was said.

The Priest reached the part of the church service where he says, "Peace be with you", and the congregation responds, "and also with you". This particular day there was a problem with the church sound system, so he stepped up to the pulpit and said, "There's something wrong with this microphone", and the congregation as conditioned to do so responded, "and also with you".

Run to Me

Some kids for whatever reason, just identify more with one parent than the other from a very young age. Jeremy was like that. He naturally seemed to be more inclined to come to me instead of his mother. This, despite the fact that while both of us shared the parenting, Margaret did much more than me.

Jeremy was about two years old. Margaret was working part time and I was working full time. We had a sitter who lived a few doors away for the days both of us were working. On our way home from work, we would stop to pick up Jeremy.

Each day Margaret and I would go to the door, shout a "hello" to our son, and each and every day Jeremy would ignore Margaret and run to greet me. While I would kid Margaret about it and she would laugh it off, I'm sure it was at least a little upsetting, as it would be for any mother.

One particular day, Margaret asked me to stay in the car while she went to the sitter's door alone to get Jeremy. He would have to run to her this time. There was no other choice.

She stepped inside the door, called his name, and he came running excitedly towards her. The only problem was he kept on running right past her, out the open door, looking around to see where I was!

Sorry Margaret.

No Privacy Here

"Are you still with us, Ryan?" I couldn't make out the muffled response. I could tell that there had been a response, I just couldn't understand what it was.

"Please try to stay still, Ryan. You have a broken leg. I know it hurts, but try not to move."

"He's in a lot of pain. Can we give him more morphine?"

The answer came from a different voice. "No, we gave him the limit for now. It'll have to wait for another half hour."

"Can someone bring another litre of blood?"

"That's seven already, so this will be number eight. Okay everyone, let's review what we've done so far."

We were in the hospital emergency department with concerns of our own. A curtain was pulled across half the area and the conversation we overheard was taking place on the other side. It occupied most of the ER staff. Did the relative calmness of the staff mean that Ryan would be alright or was it just the professional manner they went about doing their jobs?

We came to learn that Ryan had been involved in a head-on crash and had to be cut out of his vehicle by first responders before they were able to transport him to the hospital. He must have lost a lot of blood. We didn't know his last name. We didn't know where he was from, how old he was or whether he had any immediate family. We think he was young. We did however, become intimately familiar with his life-threatening medical situation.

We were praying he would survive, but all we had to base that hope on was what we could hear from the doctors and nurses. When we heard that they had stabilized him well enough to transport him to another hospital, we assumed that meant he would survive, but we didn't really know.

The last we heard he was being transported by air ambulance to a larger hospital for more specialized treatment. That's all we know. We hope he is well.

Fast Forward 15 hours

We are now in another area of the hospital. Once again, curtains are all that separate us from at least two other patients, Mary and Dominic. We have no idea what they look like, in the same way we would not recognize Ryan if we saw him.

"How do you feel about going home, Mary?", we hear a nurse ask.

"I don't know. I live alone. My eyesight is very poor and my balance is not too good. I'm afraid of falling."

"How do you manage at home if you don't see well?"

"I know where things are at home, so I can usually find them."

"I'm going to ask you a few questions, Mary. Just answer them the best you can. I'm going to list five words. After I finish saying all five words, I want you to repeat them back to me. Velvet … Cookie … Blue … Gentle … Glasses."

Mary got four out of five and with a hint, got the fifth one.

Next, Mary was asked some basic math questions. Again, she did well.

"Now Mary, when I say start, I'd like you to name as many words as you can that start with the letter "T". They cannot be numbers, places or people's names."

"How long do I have?"

"One minute."

After a slow start, Mary managed to come up with three or four words.

"Now Mary, starting at 100, I'd like you to count backwards by 7's."

After a lengthy pause, Mary said, "93". From there on it was much more difficult for her.

There was at least one more test presented to Mary. When she completed it, the nurse asked her one final question.

"Mary, can you repeat the five words that I asked you to remember when we started?"

What A Concidence!

Yikes! Unbeknownst to Mary and the nurse, on the other side of the curtain I was silently taking the test at the same time.

We learned that Mary was 89 years old. We also learned that she did very well on the test, quite possibly better than me!

Domenic was in a bed across the room diagonally. His son sat by his side. The son tried to talk to his father, but was not getting a response. The patient's breathing was labored and it sounded as though he was sleeping.

The doctor came in and observed Domenic, but she did not get a verbal response from him either.

The son said that the previous day had been similar, but at one point during the afternoon, his Dad had opened his eyes and had a conversation with him.

The doctor gently lifted Domenic's eyelids and tried to wake him. She was not successful. Next came a very difficult conversation with the son. She recounted the general condition of his father and how it had worsened. She explained that the periods of his father's awareness and his ability to communicate were lessening each day. She said that this was not a good sign. His survival for much longer was unlikely.

The son recognized the gravity of the situation, but kept referring back to the moments when his father had been lucid. "He's all I have", the son said.

The doctor consoled him as best she could, but kept referring back to the reality of the situation.

Three people we never met, but came to learn a lot about in the space of less than twenty-four hours. How did it end for them all? Well, we don't really know what happened to Ryan and we don't know if Mary made it back home or not. Sadly, we do know that Domenic passed away a couple of days later.

Where's the Rest of my Pay?

The Board of Education had an option for its teachers. Rather than receiving their full pay each pay period, they could choose to receive two thirds of what they were entitled to every pay day. This would go on for a total of three years.

They would work the first two years of the three, and take the third year off. So, after the three-year period was up, they would have worked two years and been paid for two years, but had it spread out over three.

This was a great way for those who could afford to do so to take a break for a year, whether it be to travel, look after small children, upgrade their education, or maybe just to recharge their batteries.

My mother worked in the office of a secondary school and one male teacher there decided to take advantage of this opportunity.

The three years went by without a hitch with the teacher receiving two thirds of his salary every pay period.

After returning to work and an entire fourth year passing, the teacher stopped into the office one day and told the staff that his pay deposit was incorrect. He claimed that during that fourth year, they had continued to pay him only two thirds of his salary. They had not put him back on full pay, even though he had returned to a normal work schedule.

The administrators checked into it with the payroll department, and sure enough he had been underpaid for an entire year.

Of course, the question was raised as to how this could happen, but even more puzzling was why the teacher himself had not noticed for the whole year. Had he become so accustomed to the two thirds pay he received for three years, that he totally forgot how much his true salary was? Hard to imagine.

Ultimately, the reason for his delay in reporting became evident. Not long before he informed the office of being underpaid for a year, he had removed his wife as a beneficiary. You see, his divorce was now final. Whatever settlement had been agreed upon, was obviously based on what he reported his income had been for the past four years. He could back it up with pay stubs and statements from the payroll department.

He eventually received a lump sum payment of the backpay he was owed, after the divorce settlement, of course.

I wonder if his ex-wife ever found out.

Mr. Bean?

My parents went on a number of vacations after they retired. Usually, it would be some southern locale, but one particular holiday of note took place when they visited England and met up with some members of the Sheardown clan, which was my mother's maiden name. She had contacted them through her genealogy hobby.

Mom and dad had booked a tour and decided it made a lot of sense to go to England the week prior, so they could meet up with the Sheardowns. So, after a week of visiting and informal touring with them, they were driven to the hotel where they would meet the rest of their formal tour group for the remainder of their holiday.

They got to the hotel before the group arrived and had dinner sent to their room. After eating, mom decided to go down to the lobby and wait for the tour group to arrive. Dad said he was tired and was going to have a bath and rest.

After his bath, dad decided since they were finished with what was left of the meal, he would push the cart into the hall for the hotel staff to pick up. Fresh from his bath, wearing only underwear (jockey, I assume) he opened the door and pushed the cart into the hall. He took one step too many and the door slammed behind him, locking him out of his room wearing only the jockey shorts.

So, here's this half naked 70-year-old man standing in the hall of a major hotel. He decided to hide behind a pillar as best he could. If you're having any trouble picturing this, think Mr. Bean.

Fortunately, my mom didn't stay in the lobby too long. She began to walk back along the hall to their room. Partway there she could see someone peeking out from behind a pillar, wearing underwear that looked very much like the new ones she had bought dad for the trip. After a few minutes, a hotel staff member finally came and opened the door to their room for them.

Thankfully, my sister and I were spared the expense of flying to England to bail out our father on a charge of indecent exposure.

Cat Fight

I've heard a real cat fight. It was actually a racoon and a cat on the roof of our house. A neighbor's cat showed up there one night and the racoon, who had been an uninvited guest in our attic on and off, decided to protect its territory by knocking the cat off of the roof. It was not a hot tin roof.

There was a lot of squealing and screeching, and at one point the cat was hanging by its paws from our eavestrough. The racoon won the fight, no doubt about it, but eventually I won the battle to evict it from our attic for good.

The cat fight I really wanted to describe though, actually took place in an office.

I was working as an analyst in the purchasing department at McDonnell Douglas. It was a large open concept office area that occupied most of the second floor. The rows of desks were staffed by buyers, purchasing agents, expeditors and other clerical staff. Every desk had a filing cabinet beside it, which contained copies of purchase orders and agreements.

Computers were just starting to make an appearance in offices and so this was still very much a time where hard copies of everything were printed and filed away. There were cabinets and boxes aplenty, all full of various paperwork.

My boss called me in one day and asked if I could try to find a filing stool that was used by one of the clerks, a middle-aged woman named Rose. She had gone to him and told him that it was missing.

Rose was responsible for making sure that files left on the buyer and expeditor desks were eventually filed away in the appropriate cabinet. She moved throughout the floor on a daily basis to keep up with this task.

I went to Rose and asked her about the missing stool. She immediately said, "Lillian hid it!" Lillian, was also middle-aged, but about ten years older than Rose.

Off I went to Lillian's desk to question her. Rose followed close behind.

I said to Lillian, "Do you know where Rose's stool is?"

"Yes", she replied, "I hid it. She's always leaving it lying around and I'm always tripping over it!"

Rose was now inching closer so that she could hear what Lillian was saying and she soon decided to join the conversation.

"Where's my stool?"

"I'm not telling you and you know why!"

They started to get louder and louder as they yelled back and forth at each other. Lillian stood up and faced Rose, determined not to back down.

The rest of the office staff now began to hear the raised voices and they all turned to see what the commotion was.

The two combatants were now going nose to nose and I was in the middle. Lillian made one last show of fortitude, saying to Rose that she "would NOT tell her where the stool was".

Rose was red in the face now. She leaned forward and yelled, "You b**ch!", quickly swinging her arm around at the same time and slapping Lillian across the face, sending her glasses flying.

At this point, as the designated referee, I stepped between them and ushered Rose back to a neutral corner.

Two grown women working in an office, so upset with one another that it resulted in this type of confrontation? Hard to believe.

It was the only boxing, wrestling or mixed martial arts match I ever officiated. There was no knockout recorded I'm relieved to report and a rematch was never considered.

The Frosh

The frosh or freshmen in a university dorm can get asked to do some unusual things.

In my first year, we were sent on a scavenger hunt for items around the city of Toronto, a city that most of us were not yet very familiar with. Some were easy to find, some were challenging, and some required actions that were obviously illegal.

You could get a lot of points if you brought back a fish from the Manulife Centre indoor pond. You could also get arrested, like one first year student almost did. The police let him go with a warning.

You might find yourself looking to get a TTC transfer from a specific bus/subway/street car stop with a precise time stamped on it in the wee hours of the morning. That time could be after the last bus/train/streetcar had left that particular area. Being new to the city, we wouldn't know that.

You might just need to get a coaster signed by the bartender at a specific bar. Of course, you wouldn't know what type of clientele that bar catered to until you were inside, noticed some of the other customers, and concluded that you didn't belong.

The penalty if you didn't get the required number of points on the scavenger hunt? Well, the threat was that you would be taken to some suburb and left there with nothing on except your underwear. I don't think the threat was ever carried out, but it certainly was a motivator to get as many points as you could.

One particular year, after a regular monthly meeting of the members of our residence, it was decided that the frosh would be responsible for acquiring a Christmas tree for the common room.

One of them decided that there was a tree that was just the right size they had noticed not far away. The only problem was that it was alive and well, growing in front of another residence across campus. What possible reason was that not to *acquire* it?

A group of the guys, dressed in black with saw in hand, set out one night to get the tree. They had spotters in place to warn of any approaching passersby. The tree was cut down and the ten-minute walk back to the residence began. Whenever anyone approached, they would set the tree down, pretending it was planted there while they gathered round and had a casual conversation.

They might have gotten away with the whole charade, but a university gardener/maintenance worker happened to notice a tree missing from the front of a building he looked after and that a similar looking tree showed up in the common room of our residence the same day.

All of the students who were involved had to pay for a replacement tree to be purchased and planted. They were lucky that the university administration left it at that and did not involve the police. It did turn out to be the most expensive Christmas tree they ever bought, however.

Okay, for a second time, "It's hard to believe that these are some of the business, political and academic leaders of the future".

Elevator Ride

The guys decided that Geoff might like a ride in the elevator of the girl's residence. They stripped him of his clothes, taped him to a chair, set him in the elevator and pushed the button for the sixth floor.

And for a third time, "It's hard to believe that these are some of the business, political and academic leaders of the future."

Sewer Stories

If you live in a rural area or small town, your house will undoubtedly come equipped with a septic system of some sort.

Once your town reaches a certain size, the need for a sewer system arises and when the decision to move forward is made, there is no option for homeowners. You must connect and you must arrange and pay for the link from your house to the main line running under your street.

That's the way it happened for residents of Caledon East in the 1990's. We were all inconvenienced for several months, as roads were closed completely or access was severely limited.

We chose a local contractor to make the connection to our house and when all was said and done, I'm sure he wished he hadn't taken the job.

The first mishap occurred when the person he had hired to dig the trench arrived with his backhoe. I was at work at the time, but Margaret was home with the kids.

She said that after he had been excavating for a while, the contractor came to the door and asked to use the phone. He was in a very agitated state. His face was pale and his hands were trembling as he tried to dial the number.

It was the gas company he was calling. He had accidentally punctured the gas line and needed a crew there to shut it off as soon as possible. When he went back outside to await their arrival, he screamed at the backhoe operator. He must have been oblivious to the potential severity of the situation because he was smoking a cigarette!

The emergency crew shut off the gas. The line was repaired and what could have been a disastrous situation was avoided.

Mishap number two happened a couple of days later. Again, I was at work, but Margaret was home. This time the backhoe operator had finished the majority of the digging and was watching as the contractor started to lay the pipes along the bottom of the trench, which was about 6-8 feet deep.

The soil in our area is very sandy and a hole this deep, for safety purposes should have had some sort of bracing along its walls to prevent the sides from caving in. For whatever reason, the contractor thought it wasn't necessary.

All of a sudden, the earth along the sides of the trench began to collapse and the soil came pouring in on the contractor, burying him alive.

The backhoe operator jumped from his vehicle and began frantically digging with his hands to rescue him. Every second counted now. He managed to paw away enough dirt to expose the contractor's head and allow him to breathe.

Fortunately, he had reacted quickly enough and the entire wall had not collapsed, so that he was able to continue to dig and eventually pull his colleague to safety.

There was a lot of coughing and spitting, and he was covered in dirt from head to toe. This time when he knocked on our door, it was to ask my wife for some water. He took the rest of the day off.

Mishap number three. It was a Friday when the job was finally completed. The hookup had been done and tested, and the large trench in our lawn that had extended from our front door to the road had been backfilled. It would be up to us to do any landscaping.

On the following Sunday, we went to visit Margaret's parents. When we returned in the late afternoon, I went into the house and turned on the kitchen faucet. There was water coming out of it, but there was very little pressure.

I was puzzled as to why this would be, so I went down to the laundry room and checked around the rest of the house to see if there were other taps left on, that were somehow using much of the available water flow. Nothing was amiss.

I went back to the front of the house and glanced out the living room window. There was a geyser on our front lawn! Water was shooting upwards in a line extending ten or twelve feet high, right up through the middle of the lawn!

What A Concidence!

Quickly I found the contractor's phone number and called him. He wasn't home his son explained. He was in Toronto. I told the son what was happening and asked him to get in touch with his father right away.

A short time later another local contractor happened to drive by. Fortunately, he had a tool with him that he could turn the water supply off at the road.

When my own contractor finally arrived, he said that they must have accidentally damaged the waterline while installing the sewer connection. It wasn't enough to cause a problem immediately, but the pipe had eventually burst.

So, we did without water for the rest of that day, and the next day the backhoe operator was back again to re-dig the trench, repair the waterline and fill everything back in again.

The gas line, the water pipe and the front lawn have been relatively normal ever since. Touch wood.

That's Covered by Insurance, Right?

Margaret used to work in the insurance industry. She was a Claims Manager. She had some interesting cases over the years, but this one wasn't hers.

This file belonged to a colleague. It certainly was an interesting one and the story goes something like this.

A man, age unknown, went out for the night to a bar. I don't know if this was a regular occurrence for this fellow, but it very well might have been.

I also don't know if he drank to excess often, but on this particular night he certainly did. The good news is he didn't attempt to drive home. After a full night of drinking, he took the bus.

Later, when he got off of the bus in the wee hours of the morning, he proceeded to walk the rest of the way home. He didn't make it.

The amount of alcohol he had consumed caught up with him and he passed out. He was still about a block from home, lying crossways on a driveway in front of someone else's home.

The owner of this particular house had a job that required him to be up very early in the morning, before sunrise.

After a very abbreviated morning routine, he went out the door, hopped in his car and turned on the ignition. He put the vehicle in reverse and began to back out of his driveway. After a second or two while backing up he thought he felt a clunk, almost as if he had run over something. So, he braked, put the car in drive and pulled forward a bit only to hear the clunk again.

He put the car in park and opened the driver's side door. Glancing down, he was shocked to see a man's head sticking out from under his vehicle. A quick 911 call resulted in emergency vehicles arriving very soon after.

The drunken *trespasser* went on to survive this ordeal, but he suffered very serious injuries and was hospitalized for a long time.

The driver of the car was understandably traumatized by the incident as well. Imagine how much worse he felt, when the drunk who had passed out in his driveway decided to sue him.

Did he have a case? Well, apparently so. The driver did not take proper precautions before reversing his car. He did not walk around the vehicle to ensure there were no obstacles in his path, ensuring it was safe to get in his car, reverse out of his driveway and drive to work.

This case eventually was settled out of court. I don't know what kind of settlement resulted. I do know that I have just as much or more compassion for the driver, as I do for the drunken victim who ended up with permanent, debilitating injuries.

Now, What do I do?

It was the end of another day at work and as I gathered my things to leave the office, I couldn't find my car keys. I checked all through and around my desk, all possible pockets and anywhere else I could think of. No luck.

In those days they were actual keys, the kind that have to be inserted in the lock, not the remote keys we all have today that open your car with a touch of a button.

Next place to check would be the car itself.

Maybe I locked them in the car when I arrived in the morning. After the trek to the parking lot, I glanced in the driver's side window and sure enough, there they were in the ignition, with all the doors locked. What to do now?

I started to walk back towards the office to get a coat hanger. I would try to push it in between the frame and the window and then unlatch the door.

On the way I passed Luc, who worked in my department. I told him what had happened and he asked what kind of car I drove. When I told him, he pulled out his wallet and extracted a key. "Here", he said, "I used to drive a Ford, try this".

I walked back to my car, placed the key in the lock, turned it and the door opened! I couldn't believe it. What were the odds? Not just the odds of another key opening my car, but the odds of someone having the key with them, even though they didn't even own a Ford anymore and being there, right there, when I needed it! A lucky coincidence no doubt.

Should I be happy about my good luck or should I be more concerned with the security of my vehicle?

A Bend in the arm

The school had been trying to reach either my wife or myself. The secretary said our daughter, who was 8 years old at the time, had fallen and had a "bend in her arm".

They managed to contact me first, but Margaret ended up getting to the school first. And yes, Laura had a bend in her arm. This was not a broken arm that required an x-ray to detect. This was an arm that contained a bone between the wrist and the elbow that no longer followed a straight line. Margaret remained calm, probably because Laura was so calm.

When Margaret walked into the school, Laura said "Hi Mom!" Perhaps she was in shock, because it was hard to imagine her not being in a lot of pain with a break that bad.

Usually, it's parents who have to keep their kids calm. In this case it worked the other way around.

Anyway, we took her to the hospital. The doctor sedated her, set her broken arm and ended up recommending that she stay in the hospital overnight, and then a second night for more observation.

The arm healed fine, but piano lessons came to an end never to be resumed, so Laura was probably happy about that.

Roger for Coach

Letter number two to Harold Ballard provided more advice. This time it wasn't about a player they should keep. It was about a coach they should hire.

The Toronto Maple Leafs had just finished another disappointing season and the rumor was that they would not rehire their coach, Red Kelly.

If this were to happen, I knew who I wanted their next coach to be.

Roger Neilson had just finished a season of coaching a minor league hockey team in Dallas. Prior to that he had earned a reputation for being a real innovator as Head Coach of the Peterborough Petes of the Ontario Hockey League.

Let me make it clear that I, like most Leaf fans at the time, was not impressed with the way that Ballard was running the team. My letter to him this time however, was positive in all respects. I did not call for the firing of Red Kelly, but instead suggested that should they choose to hire a new coach, Neilson was their man.

I had followed Roger's career for a few years when a cousin of mine had played for him in Peterborough. Neilson was a former high school teacher who brought those skills with him to the hockey rink. I saw him as intelligent, respected, successful and his style of defense first even fit what was traditionally a trademark of Toronto Maple Leaf teams.

So, I made all my points in my letter and mailed it off.

Harold Ballard did not disappoint me. In fact, once again he took the time to send me a personal response that addressed everything I had mentioned in mine to him. He praised me for being so positive, agreed with my assessment of Roger Neilson and assured me that should they decide to seek a new coach, Roger would be given serious consideration. He went on to say he would keep my letter on hand as they began post-season meetings and planning for the coming hockey season. Now, I really doubt he did that, but what the heck, I was thrilled.

Imagine how even more elated I was, when a few months later they actually hired Roger Neilson! Perhaps Mr. Ballard accepted advice from every fan who took the time to write him and that might explain why the team was so dreadful for so long, especially after Neilson left the team a few years later. I doubt my letter played any part in the ultimate decision to hire Roger Neilson, but I framed the response and had it hanging on my wall for several years.

Shouldn't I have received some sort of finder's fee from the Maple Leafs or a percentage of Neilson's salary for acting informally as his agent?

What A Concidence!

Letter from former Toronto Maple Leaf President Harold Ballard

MAPLE LEAF GARDENS LIMITED
60 CARLTON STREET, TORONTO, ONTARIO M5B 1L1 · (416) 368-1641

OFFICE OF
PRESIDENT, GENERAL MANAGER
AND
CHIEF EXECUTIVE OFFICER
HAROLD E. BALLARD

April 27, 1977

Mr. Larry Proctor
Box 42
Caledon East, Ontario

Dear Mr. Proctor:

    It is not often that I have the pleasure of reading such an interesting, informative letter. Your suggestions prove you to be a very knowledgeable hockey man, and the fact that any critisism you voiced was of the constructive kind, shows you to be a Leaf fan of the best sort.

    On the occasions that I have spoken with Roger Neilson, I must say that I agree with your statement that he is a very well-spoken man and a very impressive hockey coach. As you said, his record speaks for itself. If it should be decided to find a new coach you may be assured that Mr. Neilson is being kept in mind and will be given much consideration.

    You can also be assured I will be keeping your letter close at hand as the end-of-season meetings get under way here in the office.

    May I again thank you for the time you took to write. After so many letters that complain about one thing or another, your letter is a very welcome exception to the rule. We really appreciate your interest.

With kindest personal regards,

Yours truly,

HAROLD E. BALLARD
PRESIDENT

HEB:pg

Why We Are Who We Are

Do you ever try to analyze your own personality and how it evolved? What events impacted or shaped the person you are today?

I attended a small school in a small town. I was relatively successful in elementary school. I guess you could say that some of us were like the big fish in the little pond. This was good for the development of one's self-confidence. I gravitated towards leadership roles when there was an opportunity and enjoyed it. I didn't mind being noticed, as long as it was for the right reasons.

So why all of a sudden in high school, was I a much more reserved, shy person?

Well, now I was attending a much larger school in a much larger town. A little fish in a big pond. You could be noticed for a number of reasons, not all of them necessarily good. It was much safer to become the quiet one in the back.

It's not that I didn't become involved in any extra-curricular activities. There was the school band for a while, football, some sports officiating, track & field competitions, and briefly even the chess club.

They weren't the prominent roles I had in elementary school though. I was now more content to be the average non-descript guy. I remember receiving my physics exam back from my teacher in Grade 11, and as he handed it to me, I heard him say, "So that's Larry Proctor!" I had been in his class all semester and he didn't know me!

Don, one of my former managers, once said, "Not everyone can be a superstar". He was referring to employees like me! While some others may have experienced meteoric rises in their careers, I was just a stable, reliable employee, rarely missing work, never being late, doing my job consistently. Don was making the point that a well-functioning company needed both types to be successful. So, it's okay to be average!

So, how and why do our personalities evolve? Sometimes there are catastrophic events that cause changes. Other times a series of lesser things result in a gradual change. I've always believed that self-confidence is something that requires a number of successes over time to build, but one perceived failure can cause it to come crashing down.

Almost everyone can come up with some stories of their own that built them up or brought them down.

The Not-So-Amazing Race

Something I always looked forward to in elementary school was Track & Field Day. It took place sometime in May or June each year and consisted of several different competitive events.

Depending on what grade you were in, the events you could enter varied. In the primary grades, there were events like the sack race, the wheelbarrow race and a 50 yard or meter (depending on your era) dash. By the time you got to the 7th or 8th grade, the more traditional track & field competitions were contested; high jump, long jump, standing broad jump, and races of varying lengths.

In the first grade, there were four events I could enter and I happened to win them all. I had a string of successes on Track and Field Day in the years to follow, always winning at least two or three events.

The competition I was best at was the 100-yard dash. We use the metric system now of course, but back then, all the distances were measured in yards.

I was a sprinter, not much endurance, but fast for a short time. In fact, I had never lost a sprint, whether it was just playing around with friends, or an actual school competition. I always won and so I came to expect to win. My confidence level was understandably high.

As my elementary school years were coming to a close, I anticipated graduating from Grade 8 and moving on to high school. I also eagerly anticipated the final Field Day I would participate in.

When the day arrived, I was doing well in all of the events, but the 100-yard dash was yet to come.

Not that anyone asked, nor did I ever speak of winning, but of course I expected to. After all, I had never lost a Track & Field Day sprint.

We took our positions at the starting line, the starter barked his instructions and off we went.

There were a few other runners ahead of me initially, but that wasn't unusual. I wasn't the fastest starter, but with my long legs I had always been able to make up that ground.

At the mid-point of the race, I had overtaken everyone except for two runners, both coincidentally named Chris. I continued to push myself, going as fast as I could, legs churning, head steady, eyes looking straight ahead right through to the finish line and ….. a third-place finish!

Third place! I was supposed to win this race. I had always won this race.

It wasn't that Chris and Chris were new to the school. I had raced and beaten them several times in the past. Maybe they had been secretly practicing, while I had not. I'm not sure what happened, but they were definitely the better runners on that particular day.

This was one of those examples where I think one event had a resounding negative effect on my self-confidence. As a young teen, it took a real beating that day. Now, it was only a race and I didn't dwell on it for too long at the time, but years later when I look back on events that shaped my life and the personality that evolved, that 100-yard dash race on Track and Field Day in the eighth grade was probably a significant one.

On Stage Alone, in Front of a Crowd

"Are you cold?", the teacher beside me asked.

"No, I'm okay."

The reason my leg was shaking was not because I was cold. It was because I was nervous, nervous because it would soon be my turn to walk up on stage and speak.

This was a public speaking contest. All students in the senior elementary grades had to write a speech and recite it in front of the other classes and teachers. Some were then chosen to represent the school in a competition against other schools. I was one of the lucky ones.

Once on stage, the nervousness tended to lessen as the speech progressed. It was the waiting that was nerve-wracking.

We were all told that we had to memorize our speeches. The contest would be held in an auditorium at another competing school. Other students, teachers, parents, and of course the judges, would be there.

The topic of my speech was Louis Cyr, a Canadian strong man of the late 1800's who never lost a challenge. I wrote it, read it and recited it repeatedly until I had it down pat, or so I thought.

A few days before the competition, we were told that we could carry notes with us on stage. We didn't have to totally memorize our speech. By this time, I had decided I knew mine well enough that notes were not necessary. What a mistake!

Once my turn to speak arrived, I launched into my speech. Perhaps I spoke a little too quickly, the nerves taking over, but I settled into my routine and carried on.

Then it happened. At some point, a couple of minutes into my speech, for some unknown reason, maybe I was distracted by something, maybe I was saying the words but not really hearing what I was saying, who knows what it was, but I forgot my speech.

I got to a point and couldn't remember what was next, and I had no notes to refer to.

I was quiet. The audience was quiet. I expect many of them were as uncomfortable as I was, squirming in their seats while watching the 13-year-old alone on stage.

I looked up. I looked left and right trying to jog my memory, but mostly I looked down, embarrassed about the predicament I was in. I concentrated as hard as I could. Finally, it came back to me. I picked up where I'd left off and carried on, finishing without further incident.

When I returned to my seat, I asked the student beside me if the silence was actually as long as it had seemed to me. When he answered in the affirmative, I felt even more dejected. I was hoping it had only seemed like a long time to me on stage, but I guess that was not the case.

Well, needless to say I didn't win that public speaking contest. It undoubtedly knocked my self-confidence down a couple of rungs. No doubt it contributed to the type of personality I took with me to high school the next year, the quiet kid sitting in the back.

The Raid

Maybe it's a late teen, guy thing, but there's an aura of excitement and anticipation surrounding a meticulously planned and executed attack. The enemy can be real or they may just be a perceived adversary.

I'm not sure what started the confrontation. I only know that it escalated over time. Someone from St. Mikes played a practical joke on someone from VIC or vice versa, and the revenge prank definitely raised the stakes. Each successive payback scheme could less and less be referred to as just a prank.

The ultimate revenge was masterminded by the VIC guys and scheduled to take place on a Sunday evening, after dark.

I'd better insert my disclaimer here. I was not involved!

The local hydro authorities had sent a communication out indicating that there was a planned power outage for the area that would last from 10:00 pm Sunday night until 4:00 am Monday morning. The sun would have set. No lights would be on in the vicinity, resulting in a kind of eerie atmosphere settling in, or perhaps unsettling would be a more apt description. It made it a perfect time for the raid!

The Victoria College Men's Residence backed onto the St. Michael's College building. The St. Mike's building housed some faculty offices, as well as a student dormitory. A narrow parking lot was all that separated the two structures.

The St. Mike's building would be locked, but plans were made to gain access.

Some female students were recruited by the VIC guys to ring the door buzzer and request access. They were permitted to enter on the pretense that they were delivering an essay to a professor's office in the building. No one suspected anything sinister.

Once in the building, the girls let their male comrades in through a side entrance. The guys, armed with homemade smoke bombs and stink bombs, made their way to floors that contained the student residence rooms. They quietly went through the halls, into some of the washrooms, set up and set off their cache of *bombs*, then quickly left the building.

Before long, the smoke and the stench made its way through the halls and into the St. Mike's student's rooms. They all rushed to open their windows.

The VIC student's windows across the parking lot were already open. The water balloons were already prepared. The assault began.

The makeshift catapult was a slingshot device that consisted of the funnel end of a plastic Javex bleach bottle that had been cut in half, and was connected to two pieces of elastic surgical tubing. It required three people to operate efficiently. Two of them would each grab and hold tightly to an end of the surgical tubing, while the third person, the *gunner*, would pull back on the half Javex bottle. Once the maximum tension had been created by pulling back on the bottle and stretching the surgical tubing to its limit, the *gunner* would place a water balloon in the cupped side of the half bottle. When he released it, it would sling the water balloon rapidly towards its target.

I first saw these slingshot devices, referred to as *funnelators*, at the varsity football games. Students in the stands used them to sling water balloons across the field. They were powerful enough to reach the stands on the other side of the stadium. As a matter of fact, I received an indirect hit from one while working as a sideline reporter for the student radio station at a U of T football game.

Back to the story of The Raid. Some of the better aimed balloons actually flew from the Victoria College Residence through the open windows of that St. Mike's building across the parking lot. Others exploded against the wall and dripped down the exterior.

Perhaps this would have been looked at as a harmless prank, executed by some college students who were letting off steam before their final exams. The problem was, some of the balloons contained more than water. Some had been filled with a mixture of paint and water.

The next day the results were there for all to plainly see. Not only were there remnants of broken water balloons scattered throughout the parking

What A Concidence!

lot, the exterior of the St. Mike's building had multicolored blotches of paint streaking down its stone exterior.

The war between the two residences ended that night. I'm not sure if any of the guilty were found out by the university administrators, and if so, what the penalty was.

I do know the paint remained on the wall as a temporary reminder of what had occurred until the following summer, when it was finally sandblasted away.

You'll be familiar with this next quote which appears at the end of some of the other university days stories in this book.

"It's hard to believe that here in this room, are many of the business, political and academic leaders of tomorrow".

More Activities of the Leaders of Tomorrow

Some of the things that I've already mentioned that our future leaders did while in university were not what one would expect, especially considering how mature and successful I'm sure they've all become.

Here are some more of those student activities.

Sneak up on another guy and squirt him with a water pistol right in the crotch, soaking his pants in that area. This was seen to be especially humorous if the victim was just about to go to class or out on a date.

Have huge water fights in the dormitory using garbage pails full of water. Soaking each other and everything in the halls to the point where the water streamed down the stairs from the fourth floor to the basement.

Mop up that water before any administrator could notice the next morning.

Ask respected members of society to be honorary members of the student residence. Examples included Xavier Hollander (aka The Happy Hooker), Paul Rimstead (Toronto Sun Columnist who wrote one sentence paragraphs, dictated his articles over the phone and was known to enjoy a cocktail or two), and Carl Holman (spokesperson at the time for Carlsberg Beer. We were hoping he'd bring us a few free cases of beer and he did!).

Fart in an empty jar. Put the lid on it and leave it on your shelf for a few weeks. When someone asks what it is, invite them to open it, take a whiff and see if they can guess.

A slightly different version of the above. Fart while holding a needleless syringe in the vicinity of one's posterior and extract the odor into the syringe. Expel the gas from the syringe into the face of a fellow student.

Streaking – prevalent in the mid to late 1970's – This involved running through a public space naked. John decided to put his own spin on it. He would cycle naked, along Charles Street, south on Bay, make his way over to Queen's Park Crescent/University Avenue and then pedal north back to the Victoria College Men's Residence where he had started. A trial run, fully clothed, was accomplished without incident. The naked version caught a lot of motorists by surprise. No traffic accidents resulted, but John's time to do the circuit was a full two minutes faster!

Challenge another intramural hockey team to a special game. Since it was in the 1970's, at a time when several of the Canada versus Russia hockey series were being contested, it was decided our game should look as similar to those international matches as possible. Therefore, as was the custom, the national anthems of both countries were played before the game. We also exchanged gifts while on the ice, which was a tradition as well.

Since our team name was the Fishheads, we skated over and gave each of our opponents a sardine wrapped in tinfoil. They gave us a condom; no explanation was provided.

Snow Wall & Santa's Rough Day

What else do university students do in their spare time? After a large snowfall, they block the entrance to the courtyard. Some probably went on to earn engineering degrees.

Someone from the men's residence played Santa each year. Some also partied too much when they did.

Oh, my Deer!

So, there I was, on a Friday night on the afternoon shift of my summer job as a security guard for the aircraft manufacturer McDonnell Douglas, which later became Boeing.

The bulk of the employees were on the day shift and they were streaming out to their cars in the parking lot to head home for the weekend. Most of the afternoon shift was already on the job.

The company, which was located near the Toronto airport, bordered on some vacant land that contained some lightly wooded areas.

One of the departing employees came back to the guardhouse and informed us that a deer had somehow gotten into our south parking lot and was unable to find its way out. It was trying to jump the fence which was simply too high. In trying to do so, it was injuring itself.

Nobody was sure how the deer had managed to get into the parking lot in the first place, since the highway ran along the east side of the property and the other perimeters were fenced. In any case we weren't sure what to do, so we called the Humane Society. They had assisted in the past when we had problems with raccoons or other small animals in an office or manufacturing building.

The Humane Society truck arrived and started to slowly drive along beside the deer leading it along the fence line. However, this in fact was taking the deer farther away from the open land it must have come from and closer to our buildings.

The deer was now starting to bleed more from the cuts it was sustaining each time it tried to jump or barge through the fence.

I was leaning on the counter of the main guardhouse, but could not see what was taking place a few hundred meters away. Both doors were propped open, since it was a hot summer day.

The next thing I knew, I heard the clomping of the deer's feet approaching. It was now obviously in a panicked state and looking for any way out of its predicament. It bolted through one open door of the guardhouse and out the other, a couple of feet in front of me. Now it was off on a journey through the manufacturing plant where the doors were also all propped open.

Up and down the aisles it ran, the Humane Society personnel and several security guards trying to keep track of where it was. Bemused afternoon shift employees glanced up from their work, unable to believe their eyes. This lasted for close to half an hour.

Eventually a Lands and Forests official arrived and tranquillized the deer. He was quite upset with the Humane Society people for even attempting to corral it. They thought if they tried to direct the deer along the fence line, they would be able to lead it back to open land. The deer started out going in the wrong direction however and they were never able to get it turned around.

It certainly provided us with a most unusual day at work, but sadly, the deer lost so much blood that it did not survive.

Telemarketers

How many times a week do you get a call from a duct cleaning company? That or someone trying to sell windows and doors are the calls we receive most frequently from telemarketers.

How do you deal with them? Do you just hang up? Do you swear at them?

If they're selling the newest in windows and doors, they may explain the merits of the security and protection they provide. In that case, if you're Margaret, you yell at them that you "don't need any protection."

Bruce, a former neighbor, would tell them he didn't have any windows or doors in his house. Could they please send someone to rescue him? He was trapped inside and couldn't get out.

And then there was Theresa. She dealt with all telemarketers in the same way. She kept a whistle beside her phone. As soon as she received a call, she would pick up the whistle and blow it as loudly as she could right into the phone! Then she'd hang up.

The Second Time Around Interview

Quite frankly it was a telephone call I never expected to receive. I had worked at McDonnell Douglas Aircraft for 15 years when I got laid off. It was now close to four years later and they asked if I would be interested in returning.

The aircraft industry tended to be very cyclical in nature. There were always ups and downs, but the company had reduced its employment so drastically this most recent time, that most former employees never returned and I was one who never expected to get the chance.

The dilemma was that I was now working in a totally different field and for a government organization (Adult Education wing of the Peel District School Board) as opposed to a private industry. It was a change that had proven to be refreshing at that point in my life. Did I really want to go back to a manufacturing company? The fact that my current job was a contract position, while the offer to go back to McDonnell Douglas as a financial analyst again was permanent, with all previous service and benefits intact, was the main reason I felt I had to go for it.

Many management faces had changed while I was away and the interview where I would have to make a favorable impression, was with the new Director of Finance. He was an American who had recently been assigned to the Toronto office. He had only been there for a few weeks and was looking to remedy what he saw as an under-staffed department. The easiest way to do this would be to bring back former employees. They wouldn't require much training before they would be able to begin making a contribution.

My job with the Board of Education as a Career & Skills Assessment Counsellor involved presenting workshops, and working with individuals in all aspects of their own job search. Everything from administering occupational interests and ability tests to resume writing, and of course, interview skills.

I was now about to utilize some of the same tips that I had learned and had helped others with, in my own job interview.

I headed off to my scheduled appointment, armed with as much as I could remember about how to be the candidate that an employer was looking for. Even though I'd worked for the company before, this interview was with someone who I'd never met and I wanted to be as prepared and as professional as possible.

The meeting started typically. During the introductions I was conscious of maintaining good posture and listening attentively.

The Director perused my resume. He noted the various tasks and contributions I had made to the organization in the past, but he really hadn't asked me a question yet.

When he finally did ask one, it wasn't what I expected or prepared for or had ever encountered in a job interview before.

He pulled out a newspaper and opened it to the real estate listings page. He then asked me where I thought would be a good place to live in the area. He had not yet moved his family from the U.S. and wanted some local advice, I guess.

I have never been asked for real estate advice in the course of a job interview before or since.

By the way, I did get the job, so I returned to McDonnell Douglas Canada which became Boeing Toronto not long after that and I spent another nine years with them.

Job Search

I've come across many different strategies for doing a job search. Having been on both sides, doing my own search and at other times helping others with theirs, I recall what some candidates did to help them stand out from the crowd.

If a hundred or more resumes pass the desk of the hiring manager, as was the case in at least one of the positions I applied for, how can you increase your chances of being noticed?

It depends on the nature of the job of course. You couldn't use this strategy for business related positions, but here are some ways that applicants I have heard about got the attention they wanted by uniquely tailoring their resumes.

Sent their resume in a tennis ball can when applying for a recreation job. When mixed in with other resumes in standard envelopes, guess which one the hiring manager opened first?

Structured their resume like a menu when applying for a restaurant industry position. It contained *Appetizers, Entrees and Desserts*.

Included in their list of Interests, Activities & Interesting Facts was a note that they were a former classmate of Ivana Trump. When critiquing this candidate's resume, I said I didn't think it was appropriate to include that on a resume. He replied he wanted to leave it as it was, because it was often the first thing the interviewer commented on in the course of a job interview. It acted as a real ice breaker. Good enough reason for me!

As far as telephone interviews go, do them standing up. Your voice will project better.

You have to get outside of your comfort zone at times. Cold calling is not something many people are comfortable with, but it's surprising who you may get to talk to. I fully expected to be headed off by secretaries or administrative assistants, but was surprised to get through to a VP of the National Hockey League and a VP of the Toronto Blue Jays during my job search. I didn't get jobs with either of those organizations, but it built some self-confidence just to be able to talk to them.

When you get to the interview stage, there are the obvious tips that most of us are aware of. Dress appropriately, have a firm handshake and make eye contact with each of those interviewing you.

Remember, they want to hear what you've accomplished. They don't want to listen to you rhyme off a list of the positive attributes you think you have. They want you to tell them the stories that demonstrate those positive characteristics.

Remember to describe the situation you were in, describe the action you took and the result that occurred. You'll score a point on the interviewer's tally sheet each time that you do.

Even though you are not likely to know what specific questions they will ask, go into the interview with a few of your most positive stories in mind and try to include them in your responses.

When my final stint at McDonnell Douglas Canada/Boeing Toronto ended, I had been there a total of 24 years, 15 the first time around and another 9 years when I returned from 4 years working elsewhere.

I had applied for a position at Humber College after leaving Boeing and I got a call to go for an interview. One of the questions I was asked, was to describe my previous experience. I told them about my first 15 years work experience at MDCAN and how there had been a large layoff, which is why I had left the first time.

Any prospective employer quite naturally will be interested in the reasons why a candidate left a previous job. Was it for a promotion? Were they let go for job performance reasons? It's not always apparent from a resume. The candidate must demonstrate that it had nothing to do with their own personal skills or quality of work.

I indicated that my layoff was due to the fact that there was a decline in the sales of the aircraft being manufactured, so the company had to reduce their workforce accordingly. I also told them that four years after being laid off, they called me and asked me if I would be interested in returning.

Would they have done so if there had been issues with my job performance or my attendance, or anything else in the past? No, of course not.

By making sure that I told the interview team, that I had been asked to return to my former company, I demonstrated that management had some level of trust and comfort with me.

I went on to further describe my role when I returned to MDCAN/Boeing for the final 9 years. I told them that the more recent layoff was as a result of the company closing its Toronto area facility.

I also said one more thing. I wasn't asked about this, but I made sure I concluded my answer to their question by saying, that in my total of 24 years with the company, there had been as many as approximately 5,000 employees at its peak and when I left, there were only 10.

All of this was true, but once again that statement could only lead them to infer positive things. It could demonstrate versatility, reliability, trustworthiness and probably someone who was a good team player. I never had to mention those qualities myself. The story validated them.

Oh, Christmas Tree

Pam and Marie were coworkers, a few years younger than me. I was a single guy in my 20's, with no steady girlfriend at the time. Pam and Marie had become friends of mine through work. We really didn't socialize outside of the workplace, unless it was some sort of company function.

I lived by myself in a house I'd recently purchased and my parents lived nearby. Christmas was celebrated at their place, so I explained to Pam and Marie that I did not bother with a Christmas tree or any other decorations in my house. Why would I bother, since I lived by myself anyway?

I didn't think twice about it, but it seemed to be more of an issue for Pam and Marie than it was for me.

"You've got to have a Christmas tree!" they exclaimed. "It just wouldn't be the same without one."

"But, why?" I replied. "I won't be at home for Christmas anyway. It's not worth the effort."

A few days before Christmas, there was a knock at my door. There stood Pam and Marie. They hadn't asked if I'd be at home or anything. They just took a chance and showed up unannounced.

"Go upstairs and stay there until we tell you to come down", they said.

I followed their instructions and waited patiently.

About 10 minutes later they called me to come down to the family room.

Sitting on the floor in one corner of the room was a small Christmas tree decorated with some tinsel and a few small ornaments. They hadn't gone out and spent lavishly on the decorations or anything, but they had taken the time to gather whatever they had available between the two of them and decorate what was now my Christmas tree.

Larry Proctor

Some holidays you may give or receive a gift that makes that year more memorable than others. That particular Christmas was one for me.

P.S. – The best gift my sister and I ever gave our parents when we were quite young, was a toaster. However, we were a little worried that they had already requested it be set aside for them when we saw it on the shelf of the local hardware store. It had the PROCTOR name engraved on it. I guess we were too young to know that Proctor-Silex manufactured toasters.

Quotes by People I Know

John (a former fellow employee) – "I was almost Pierce Brosnan's father."
"Huh?", we all said.

Explanation –John explained that when he lived in Ireland, he used to date the woman who eventually became Pierce Brosnan's mother, so conceivably, no pun intended, if the relationship had continued, he could have been Pierce's father.

Shirley (another former fellow employee) – "If I have known someone for a while and we start dating, I believe it's okay to sleep with that person after the third date."

Response from a guy who overheard her – "What are you doing Monday, Tuesday and Wednesday?"

Doug (my father) – "I only dated teachers, because they made you do it over and over again until you got it right."

Explanation – None required.

Stan (friend) – After receiving a tube of Preparation H as a gag gift, he said, "I've tried this stuff and for all the good it does, you might as well shove it up your ass."

Explanation – None required unless you don't know what Preparation H is.

Hal (former secondary school Principal) – While visiting Wales with his school's rugby team, and after a match against the local side, they socialized together and enjoyed some of the town's musical talent. After the performance, Principal Hal naively asked a local lad how to say the word "encore" in Welsh. "I fyny eich ass", he was told.

"I fyny eich ass!", Hal yelled loudly. "I fyny eich ass!" English translation, "Up your ass! Up your ass!"

Explanation – None required, just an apology from me for two ass stories in a row.

Further follow up – Principal Hal was NOT sent to the Principal's Office.

Progressive Dinners

The only problem with progressive dinners is that everyone has to clean their house and everyone has to prepare part of the meal. They are a lot of fun though.

It's a unique way to get together with friends for dinner. The perfect number is probably four households. By the end of the day, you will have visited everyone and had a four-course meal.

At the first family's home, you start your meal with appetizers. They are free to decide what will be served. After spending an hour or so there, everyone packs up and either drives or walks (ideally), to the second home.

The second couple are responsible for soup or salad. Their own special recipes are welcome, and again after about an hour everyone moves on.

The third family has the largest responsibility as far as the meal goes. They must cook and serve the entrée.

It's also important for the couple whose home is the next stop each time, to leave a little early from the previous stop, in order to get their portion of the meal cooking and to be ready for the imminent arrival of the rest of the guests, 15-20 minutes later.

The final indulgence is dessert at the last stop of the day, and afterwards if everyone chooses, the party goes on. This is the home that everyone will likely spend the most time at, so they get to decide if there will be a curfew.

When we planned these progressive dinners with friends of ours, we added a little twist. All of the homeowners had to have a theme at their house. They would decorate and dress accordingly. The rest of us would not know the theme until we arrived.

There were some great ideas over the years. There was a French Café, with small round tables and checkered tablecloths. The hosts were dressed as waiters and served us their home-made soup.

There was the western theme, where we sat on bales of hay in the garage and were served chili by the hosts who were dressed in cowboy gear.

There was even a wedding theme, with bombonieres given to each guest and the bride wearing her wedding gown for the first time in 10 years.

To make it all work the following are essential; select food options that can be mostly prepared in advance, and limit alcohol consumption, so driving from home to home can be done safely.

Home Signs

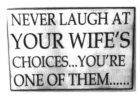

These are a few of the signs hanging in our house that are definitely truisms.

What Kind of Fruit are You?

We were in the second day of a two-day outplacement service, providing us with job search strategies and advice. We'd gone through the networking, resume writing and cover letter tips. Now we were concentrating on the job interview and more specifically, the types of questions you might expect to be asked.

We had all drafted some possible answers to the typical questions and now the facilitator was providing examples of some of the more unusual questions she had heard. Believe it or not, she said she had been told of someone being asked as part of their interview, "If you were a fruit, what kind would you be?"

I'm not sure what kind of a job they were being interviewed for and I can only assume the interviewer was trying to see how creative the person was, or maybe they wanted to measure their reaction when asked something totally unexpected.

I got to thinking that perhaps the type of fruit you choose and the reasons why, could really be a reflection of your personality.

Then I really got to thinking and decided that there was an article waiting to be written here and maybe even an entire workshop to be developed! Some people will buy anything. They love these fun little exercises that tell them what they're supposed to really be like.

So, here they are. The unofficial, *What Kind of Fruit are You?* definitions. Just read all of them and decide what you are. You are the fruit. The fruit is you.

Apple – comes in many shades and varieties. Others may view them as anything from *spies* to simply *delicious* to be with. Generally considered to be very hardy and resilient. Able to withstand outside pressures.

Banana – has very distinct look compared to others. A straight-shooting type, although most tend to throw you a mild curve. Tough on the outside and difficult to get to open up when younger, but generally become soft and even mushy as they age.

Grape – usually uniform in appearance. Tend to be better in a group situation, but sometimes break away on their own. Can truly change their character if allowed to alter their form and ferment. Then, they may produce a heady, lucid feeling. Subtle differences in their character are noticed depending on their origin.

Blueberry – very fragile and usually petite. Lots of hidden attributes/values that most others are not aware of. Easily get lost in the crowd, but once discovered they tend to be appreciated for lengthy periods of time.

Orange – very thick-skinned. Some more seedy than others. The smaller in size, the easier to peel away the outer layer and see the true inner self.

Kiwi – a complex type with several layers to interpret. Can be kind of fuzzy and plain outwardly, but when you peel that away you'll discover a much more vibrant and exciting character. The inner core/self is different again, firm and solid and quite a contrast to the middle layer. This variety may be evidence of their versatility.

Cantaloupe – almost impossible to break through their outer shell without some kind of help. When you finally do however, they are usually soft and sweet and well worth getting to know. Sometimes they don't last very long. Their staying power is not the best.

Lemon – associated with failure or below acceptable standards. They are very bitter deep inside, although they try to conceal this with their outer appearance. Can add either a mild hint or a sudden burst of excitement when combined with others that may be bland on their own.

Peach - kind of fuzzy on this one. Another who's exterior doesn't depict what's inside, soft and fleshy, with a solid core. Usually, they're thought of positively as in, "What a peach!"

Pineapple - a prickly outward appearance covers up what is a delightful and juicy inner self. Sometimes they give the impression they've descended from royalty with a crown-like appearance on top.

Fight or Flight

Morning person or evening person? In our household, I am usually the first to retire for the night. I'm also the first one to get up in the morning. Margaret usually follows about an hour or two later in both instances.

This particular night we were both a little more tired than usual, no doubt from hosting a birthday party for one of the kids that day. We were in bed relatively early and at some point, Margaret woke up and got out of bed to go to the washroom.

The next thing I knew, just as she made it to the door, she let out a muffled scream, turned around and ran back into the room. She proceeded to quickly jump from the foot of the bed onto the mattress beside me.

Now I couldn't remember her ever coming to bed with that much enthusiasm before, so I knew something was wrong.

"There's someone in the hall, coming up the stairs", she managed to whisper.

I got out of bed slowly and as my eyes adjusted to the darkness, I was sure that there was no one in the stairwell. However, a little remnant from the birthday party was.

One of the helium-filled balloons from the party that we'd left in the family room, had started to float up the stairs. A balloon, when seen by someone half asleep in less than perfect light in the middle of the night, sure looked like an approaching human head. It was enough to scare the dickens out of them!

Mind Games

The course was called "The Science Fiction Novel". The choice was to write an essay on a science fiction topic or write a science fiction story.

One required research, the other allowed you to just use your imagination. I chose the latter.

My science fiction story was titled "Mind Games", the Hunger Games came much later and was written by someone else.

Mind Games was a battle of the minds between two humans of the future. They were extraordinary human beings though. They had highly developed brains. They were capable of everything from extra sensory perception (ESP) to telepathy to telekinesis.

They could sense things that others couldn't; they could transfer thoughts or ideas without actually speaking them; and they could transport objects simply through mind control. The story described how they competed in a series of events that measured their abilities in each of those categories.

I don't remember what my grade was on this story, maybe a B-, probably a C+. Let's just say I never considered getting it published. I certainly didn't take it back to the professor demanding a higher mark.

While you undoubtedly have never heard of or read my short story, you may be aware of the song by the late John Lennon, also titled Mind Games.

For some reason, I decided I would imbed some of the lyrics from Lennon's song into my story. They were sprinkled throughout the tale.

My characters were "pushing the barriers, planting the seeds". They were "doing their ritual dance in the sun", were "projecting their images, in space and in time" and always had "faith in the future, outta the now".

The way this story of mine ended, was with a competition called *Tabula Rasa* between the two combatants. Tabula Rasa is a theory of personality that many psychology students would be familiar with. It basically means clean slate. It's a theory that all humans at birth have an absence of preconceived ideas or rules for processing data. We develop our own rules as we grow. Our overall personalities are formed through our own personal sensory experiences and education.

So, picture the opponents in my fictional mind competition. They are competing in the final event, Tabula Rasa, which requires them to clear their minds of everything. They are to stay in this mindless state for as long as they can. They must think of nothing. Whomever does so the longest, will be declared the winner.

They are both so skilled in mind control that neither will give in and so the game never ends. It lasts for an eternity. Their minds having been erased forever.

I ended the story with the words of John Lennon again, "Keep on playing those mind games forever, raising the spirit of peace and of love."

Kind of corny, schmaltzy, amateurish, or all of the above, and more maybe? I know. I know.

To make matters worse, the comments written by the prof on my story beside the mediocre grade he gave me were as follows: "I don't know why you chose to end your story with some lyrics from a John Lennon song. They seem out of place". He had totally missed all of the other lines of the Lennon song scattered throughout my work of fiction. He obviously didn't get it.

On the other hand, I guess if you have to explain your submission to the professor, it isn't very good. I'd have to be satisfied with the C+.

DENSA

I don't know anyone who is a member of the High IQ Society otherwise known as MENSA, or maybe I do and they just haven't told me. They might think that I'd look at them differently or I just wouldn't understand.

Apparently, the word MENSA is derived from Latin and means table, the idea being that it was a round table society. Personally, I don't care what shape the table is that we all sit around.

So, I decided DENSA was much more appropriate for me. DENSA is an acronym for the phrase "Diversely Educated Not Seriously Affected" and of course, it's a bit of a spoof of MENSA.

As a young adult, I actually attended one of the DENSA meetings several years ago, but only one I must stress. It was at the Chelsea Hotel in Toronto. The Toronto Star even sent a reporter and photographer to cover it. We made the paper.

All living creatures possess some form of intelligence, but it is only the highest forms of life that are capable of being stupid.

With a turkey as its logo, DENSA brought to light acts of stupidity. It gave them the notoriety they deserved. With so many examples to pick from, the group's motto was well chosen, "Stupidity Knows No Bounds."

It should be noted that those of us in attendance recognized our own stupidity. However, many people don't realize they are stupid, so it was our job to point it out to them. The group that repeatedly had to be reminded were politicians.

There were plans to produce a newsletter and fill it with the many examples of how stupidity has shaped history. DENSA awards of the month and the year were considered. Perhaps we could even run candidates in elections or better still, endorse stupid candidates of established political parties.

I think I still have my official DENSA button somewhere, but I don't wear it anymore like a truly dedicated, still active member would.

So why didn't I attend another meeting? It probably has something to do with that famous Groucho Marx quote, "I refuse to join any club that would have me as a member."

P.S. - When I told my father I was going to attend a DENSA meeting, he did not like the idea. He said it was stupid. I said, "Exactly!"

Strike!

I don't bowl very often, but I have gotten the occasional strike. I was never a baseball pitcher, so I never threw a strike. I did have a unique answering machine message at one time though. It went something like this.

"Larry Proctor is at the plate, there are two out and the bases are loaded. Here comes the pitch. It's a strike! Another one on its way. Strike two! The pitcher winds and delivers. Strike three! Larry Proctor is out! Yes, Larry Proctor is out. Please leave him a message after the beep."

Strikes at the workplace though are another matter. I've experienced three of them. Although I had some jobs where I was a member of a union, most of my working life I was in non-bargaining unit roles. During each of these strikes, I was a non-unionized employee, so I had to cross the picket line. There was never any violence, but at times there was definitely an uneasy feeling. Thankfully for all, none of the strikes lasted too long.

The first strike occurred while I was employed at McDonnell Douglas. I soon learned that there were two ways to get into work safely and relatively quickly.

If you are driving and there are traffic lights at the entrance to the parking lot, approach it head-on. That way, when the traffic light changes you can drive straight in. If you try to turn left or right from the road into the lot, the picketers can legally cross at the crosswalk, thus blocking the entrance to vehicular traffic, meaning only one or two cars manage to get in with each light change.

Another solution was to find parking nearby and walk to work from there. Enter through a pedestrian gate which was not as likely to be staffed by picketers.

One thing I remember doing though, was avoiding the entrance where a barrel with firewood was burning to keep the picketers warm, while one of them *stood guard* with an axe over his shoulder and a menacing look on his face.

The two strikes that occurred while I worked at Humber College, one by faculty and one by support staff, were a little different. Many of them normally worked side by side with the administrative staff. Everyone wanted to maintain solid working relationships throughout. I can recall taking food out to the strikers around lunch time or bringing them donuts in the morning.

The good news is that in all cases the strikes did not drag on too long, agreements were eventually reached and everyone was able to work together again afterwards.

Travel

Iceland, Nicaragua, Guatemala, Peru, Ecuador, Cuba, Barbados, U.S.A., South Korea, Laos, Thailand, Vietnam, Spain, Portugal, France, Germany, Italy, Monaco and Switzerland.

Can you guess what they represent? I have only visited three of them.

A vacation for Margaret and I is typically a week in the sun during the winter and more often than not it is in Jamaica.

That much larger list of countries above, are those our daughter, Laura, had visited by the time she was in her mid-twenties.

We all definitely notice some traits or tendencies that our children seem to inherit from us. There are other likes or dislikes however, that we wonder, "Where did that come from?"

The kind of travel Laura has done is not the kind her parents have done.

She visited Ecuador twice, the first time living with a local family for three months and helping at a daycare facility. Nicaragua was a school trip where they helped build a library. She spent a year in South Korea teaching elementary school.

Closer to home, she spent a summer teaching school on a First Nations Reserve in northern Ontario, which was only accessible by air.

Twice, she travelled to and from The School of the Americas in Fort Benning, Georgia, as part of several groups that go there each year to protest the training of foreign fighters.

Many of those who attend this military facility return to their native countries and utilize the military training they received to further exacerbate the human rights abuses already occurring. That can be everything from torture to rape to murder.

All of these journeys were the kind that Margaret and I looked at with some trepidation. While we admire Laura's adventurous spirit, we are content to relax on that beach in Jamaica.

The Leafponaut

As teenagers, my group of friends and I decided we would write our own sports newsletter. Now this *publication* wasn't really a newsletter as such. In today's terms you might refer to the stories it contained, as *fake news*.

The name of the periodical was the Leafponaut. We were all fans of the Toronto Maple **Leaf**s, the Montreal Ex**po**s (the only Canadian major league baseball team at the time), and the Toronto Argo**naut**s football club of the CFL.

We didn't really publish anything. In fact, there was only one copy which we passed around amongst ourselves, taking turns reading it.

I wrote the first issue which contained some semi-serious stories about our favorite teams, along with some attempts at humor. Looking through many of the issues we had created that I retrieved from the archives (a cardboard box in my closet), I can honestly say there wasn't anything very funny about any of them. At the time though ……. Well, we were all in our mid-teens, so our writing skills were still in the development stage.

There were two highlights from the total of ten issues that were eventually completed. One was the creation of the first Mexican born professional hockey player; a fictional character named Pedro Poopkins. The other highlight was the selection of the *All-Pro, Oh No!* National Hockey League team.

If you made *All-Pro, Oh No!*, you were considered to be the worst player at your position in the league. At the time the worst team in the Western Conference of the NHL was the California Golden Seals. They all wore white skates, so maybe that contributed to their poor play and the eventual demise of the franchise.

It was decided by the editor of the Leafponaut (me), that the entire squad of *All-Pro, Oh No!* players from the West, would be selected from the Golden Seals. I pored over the statistics and selected those who either had hardly played, or played but rarely scored a goal, or had hardly any other meaningful contributions.

One of the players who made my infamous list was a defenseman who I'll simply refer to as Dick M. Whether Dick M. deserved to be *All-Pro Oh No!* or not, may have been hotly debated at the time, but I doubt it. Other editors of the Leafponaut had their own lists, some included him, others did not.

Within a few years, all of those issues of the Leafponaut were in that cardboard box in the closet and even Dick M. was a distant memory, until ....

Fast Forward 8 Years

A cousin of mine was playing professional hockey and at this point, before a brief career in the NHL, he was with the Rochester Americans of the AHL. Guess who his coach was? That's right, it was Dick M.!

One year, I decided to drive to Rochester and watch my cousin play a game. It was just before the Christmas break in late December. Since there would be a few days before the next game, all of the players were invited to the coach's house for a party to celebrate the holiday season. Any players who had family and friends at the game were told that they were welcome to bring them. So naturally, I tagged along.

As I'm sitting there talking to a couple of the players, I mentioned that a few years back my friends and I had included Dick M., their current coach, on a list of the worst players in the NHL. I said it was all a bit of a joke and they found it funny, but then they suggested I tell him!! Are you kidding? No way!

Here I am, partying at Dick M.'s house, eating his food and drinking his beer. I wasn't about to tell him I thought he was a terrible hockey player. He'd never find out from me that he once made *All-Pro Oh No!*

The Hockey Coach

Prior to getting married and having kids of my own, I did some coaching, primarily baseball and hockey. Once Jeremy and Laura began to play, I gradually became involved in coaching a number of their baseball, soccer and hockey teams too.

I was coaching the Caledon Hills Lightning Pee-Wee Selects Hockey Team one year, when a parent asked to speak to me privately. He said that another boy on the same team was yelling and swearing at his son on the ice during the games.

I asked the assistant coaches, without naming names, if they were aware of the situation. None of us had ever noticed anything like this happening, either during games or practices. However, with mouth guards and face shields and the poor acoustics in most arenas, it could easily have happened without us knowing.

The kids were at that age where some of them might see swearing as a *cool* thing to do. They wouldn't do it in front of us, but amongst their peers they might talk tough. We also never had any indication that there was any friction between these two particular players or any other members of the team for that matter.

All of this presented a bit of a dilemma. A complaint had been lodged and it was probably a valid one. I didn't feel we could confront the player who had been identified as *the swearer* without direct evidence myself. However, I also thought that it most probably was happening even though we hadn't observed it, so I needed to do something to stop the behavior.

Every game I tried to have something to say to the team in the locker room before the game. It was always brief and I tried to make it easily understood and relevant. I've never understood coaches who before a game feel it's their duty to make a long-winded speech to the team. Even worse are those who feel they have to provide analysis to the team after a game is over. Kids of any age have tuned you out after the first minute, so you might as well save your breath.

The next game we played, I made a few general comments to all the players about the importance of teamwork and how they should only say positive things about their teammates. Never be critical of each other.

I then put all the names of the players on the team in a hat and went around the room asking them each to pull a name from the hat. They all had to say something positive about the player whose name they had chosen and why that person was important to the team. Also, I had secretly rigged the selection process so that the player who was accused of swearing at his teammate had in fact drawn that player's name to speak about.

All of the players came up with good things to say and the parents told me later they were happy with the way the situation had been handled. As far as I know the problem never reoccurred.

P.S. – The toughest question I ever had to answer as a coach came from one of the 12-year-old boys on the team. "Coach, what is cleavage?"

Performance Evaluation

That dreaded time of year in the business world for us all (I think), is when performance evaluations are due. What can you possibly say that you didn't say the year before, whether you're the manager or the employee?

I can't really think of a particularly memorable review I provided for any of the employees I managed. I do however, remember my favorite of the ones I received from one my bosses.

I had a new manager. As matter of fact, she was new to the company. I had worked there for a while as a financial/systems analyst. She was a manager in the purchasing department and everyone else who reported to her was either a buyer or an expeditor.

My role was unique in the department, dealing with many of the internal department-specific computer reports and systems, so it was always difficult for the director to decide just who I should report to. This time he determined it would be Mary.

I think I was the last to be called into Mary's office for my review. She had worked there less than a year and I'm sure she felt much more comfortable doing the reviews of those in the true purchasing positions. After all, her background was in supplier management, so she was at ease discussing things of that nature with buyers and expeditors alike.

Mary handed me my computer-generated printout which showed my salary increase and said "Well Larry, I don't really know what you do, but you're doing a good job!"

My friends all said it sounded like I had the perfect job!

The Effective Meeting

There are already enough books on the market and workshops available that describe how to plan and execute an effective meeting. I'm not about to try to replicate or improve on any of them.

However, I have been involved in, or personally witnessed, a few things of interest.

Some people feel that if they haven't said anything during a meeting, they must get on the record, even if they basically repeat what someone else has already said. As a result, some meetings drag on far longer than necessary. The cure for that? *The Stand-Up Meeting*.

The *Stand-Up Meeting* was used at MDCAN. It was a necessary daily morning meeting, to discuss the status of parts shortages and how it might affect the upcoming day's schedule. If these meetings dragged on, they would severely impact all those involved, delaying them from getting to the rest of the tasks they had to accomplish that day. So, the meetings were held in an area with no tables and no chairs. Everyone stood for the entire meeting. It was an effective way to limit unnecessary discussion.

Other meetings had "no cell phone" rules. You either turned them off or left them on a table outside of the meeting room before entering. Focus on the purpose of the meeting, not your latest tweet or text.

Be on time! How do you ensure that? Schedule the meeting for 7:59 a.m. That time alone is a hint in itself, so you'd better be there for the start of the meeting. Not only that, if you were late, you would find the door locked and it would not be opened for you. No one would dare be late a second time.

Having food at meetings works too, especially coffee and donuts. I actually lost weight when I retired from Humber College where it seemed most of the meetings included refreshments of some kind.

Humber also had an unofficial club known as *The Seagull Club*. It consisted of a few guys who always seemed to know where the meetings with food were. They would show up when the meeting had ended to pick through the leftovers. I don't know if they ever had to bring or buy their own lunch in all the time they worked there.

I've often thought about meetings I have attended with a group of people. When the meeting is over, you think back to what was said and what was decided. Usually, there are some people who talk more than others, while some don't speak at all.

If everyone invited is there because they have something important to contribute, then everyone should speak and listen fairly equally, right? So, look at it this way, if there are 10 people in the meeting, then everyone should speak approximately 10% of the time and listen the other 90%.

The *Skip Level Interview*. This was an interesting one. Usually, managers are tasked with evaluating their employees. This process, conducted by a neutral facilitator, worked in reverse. A group of employees were asked to comment on and critique their boss. All responses were kept confidential of course, with nothing to connect anything that was said back to the individual.

I was a facilitator for a few of these sessions. While you would expect some groups to be critical of their supervisor, I didn't find much of that at all. Most had a very good relationship with their team.

However, there was a common thread I discovered among almost all of the groups. While they almost always entirely agreed that any issues or shortcomings in their respective departments were not the fault of their immediate supervisor, they also almost always pinned the blame on their boss's boss.

The front-line staff would say that their supervisor was doing everything he or she could to correct any problems, but the managers above him or her were not.

The supervisors in their session, would then say that their manager was doing everything to help resolve issues, but the senior managers or directors above him or her could do more.

I'm not sure what any of this really means. I expect it was about everyone just trying to maintain a level of respect and good will with those that they worked closest with, and at the same time knowing that things weren't perfect, so they had to place the blame somewhere.

The Dummy Who Made us Money

I don't know how the idea originated, but it took a few twists and turns along the way and it ended up making money.

The location was the men's residence at the Victoria College Campus of the University of Toronto. The occasion was just another weekend where a few students make the trip home to visit with family, but most stay around to study, party, and relax, although not necessarily in that order. We'd catch up with those who went home for a couple of days when they returned on Sunday evening.

What prank would be devised and who would the victim be this time?

Well, the chosen victim was Desmond and the group of pranksters set about making their plans. They collected an old pair of pants, a shirt, a pair of shoes, a styrofoam ball about the size of a human head, and lots of crumpled newspaper.

They fastened the shoes to the bottom of the pant legs, sewed the top of the pants to the shirt and proceeded to stuff crumpled newspaper inside the whole thing until it somewhat resembled a human being. The styrofoam ball was attached to the collar of the shirt to top things off. They now had created something, especially if it happened to be viewed in a darkened room, which was very similar in appearance to a human body of sorts, although not a very lively one.

Sunday afternoon before he returned, they got Desmond's roommate to open his door and they proceeded to hang the body they had created by a rope from the light fixture in the middle of his room. It looked pretty limp hanging there with its head slightly askew, arms and legs dangling. The wait for Desmond's return began.

Around 8:00 p.m. word quickly spread that Desmond was seen coming up the walk to the front door of the residence. Everyone waited quietly in their own room for his reaction.

I'm not sure whether to describe it as a scream, a yelp, or a loud gasp, maybe even all three! You can imagine how startled he was to find the silhouetted *corpse* hanging from the middle of his room.

Once it was done scaring Desmond, the *body* hung around the residence for a while. It demonstrated it had a variety of uses, despite the fact it lost its styrofoam head somewhere along the way.

Quite often the headless man would be placed on the toilet of the washroom cubicle with the door locked, so that anyone entering would only see a pair of legs. A quick glance would not give anyone reason to doubt that it was a real person in there. If they wanted to use the facilities, they would always find the stall was occupied. There was only one washroom for the eight students per floor of the residence house, so they'd be forced to go to another floor if they didn't want to wait to do their business.

Speaking of business, they even found a way this *guy* could be part of a profitable venture. These were university students, so of course they came up with some very unique and creative ideas.

All you have to do is sit the dummy on the edge of a busy pedestrian walkway near the residence, hang a sign on him that says he is blind and place a cup beside him for donations. At the end of the day, you empty the cup, bring him inside and get him ready for the next day and more of the same. Easy money! No tax was ever paid on these earnings, but no fortunes were made either.

Our friend became a real member of our house that year. He was even included in our year-end photo, propped up by two students on either side of him.

P.S. – Desmond was the victim of another prank on a weekend he chose to go home and visit his family. On this occasion, another student named Chris decided he would hide under Desmond's bed and scare him when he returned.

Desmond returned late Sunday evening. Not long afterwards, he crawled into bed and pulled the covers over himself. The room was silent, but that didn't last long. After about 10 minutes, Chris, who was hiding

What A Concidence!

under the bed, slowly reached his arm up and grabbed Desmond. I'm sure the shriek and the terror anyone listening had heard was real.

The house dummy without his styrofoam head. The sign on him reads, "I am blind and have no head." I'm in the photo, top row, second from right, wearing the dark glasses.

A Letter to my Sister

When she was in her mid-twenties, my sister backpacked through Europe. She had worked a few years and decided to take a break and do some travelling. She and a friend initially went on an organized tour of several countries in Europe with a group of similarly aged, young adults.

When the tour ended her friend came back home, but Diane decided to continue the travel adventures on her own. As many people of that age do, she stayed in hostels and carried only what would fit in her backpack.

Every now and then she would send a postcard to our parents, but apart from that, they would never really know where she was. There was no internet, text messaging or cell phones in those days.

When she came back home a few months later, she had many stories to tell us, some that were funny and some that were even kind of scary.

I think one of her favorites was once when she had very little time to catch a transfer at a train station. She was moving from one European country to another and didn't have time to exchange her money (before the euro).

She had a rail pass, but there was a premium for this particular route. She knew that she would have to pay the additional fee after the train departed and she knew she wouldn't be able to do so. The alternative would have been to spend the night in the train station by herself, something she did not feel safe doing, so she decided to board the train.

When they came to collect, not only couldn't she pay, there was a language barrier. To make matters worse, no one else in her part of the train spoke English to help translate.

Guess what happened? The other passengers recognized her dilemma and they collected enough amongst themselves to pay her train fare. A small thing perhaps, but an example of human goodwill that we all can appreciate, especially in these times when it seems that the differences in our cultures are highlighted more than the similarities.

Fast Forward Two Months

Diane had been back home for a while, but was still somewhat restless. She'd met some Australians during her European adventures and they were continuing their own travels throughout North America. Would Diane like to meet up with them in Colorado and eventually work their way south to Mexico? Of course, she would!

Occasionally Diane would let Mom and Dad know where she would be staying for a while or where she would be arriving in a few days. That way if they wanted to send her a letter they could. They suggested I write to her too.

I decided to have a little fun. I started my letter off normally, then began telling little white lies and gradually had the stories get more and more bizarre.

Here's my letter to my sister.

Dear Diane,

How are you? Everything in Caledon East is fine. Not much to report. A few things have changed since you left however, so I'll just run through them.

I bought a new car, a Corvette!!

A week after I bought it, I found out I would be laid off from my job. I think I'll just play golf for a while and enjoy myself.

It won't be too bad though, because I won the lottery! Not the big prize, but $100,000 is not too shabby!

A couple of my friends and I have decided to rent a house together. Maybe it's just as well I'm moving out though, because here's the big news.

Last week we were all outside on a gorgeous night. We looked up and the house was on fire! Half of it was burned pretty badly, so we're living in the other half. Your room is completely gone!

It's too bad because dad had just agreed to rent it out. He said whoever the new tenant was, they would likely keep the room a lot neater than you did.

What A Concidence!

Soon after the fire, mom and dad started to fight a lot (even more than before). They separated for a week when dad came home from work one day and found that mom had sold the dog and used the money to buy a new couch! Dad said, "We have too much damn furniture!"

They can't even agree on who gets neighbor George as their lawyer. So, he's representing them both! He'll make a bundle off of them.

Well, I guess I'd better go for now. Hope your life has been more exciting than ours. Caledon East is a pretty dull place to live.

Your brother,
Fred Jackson
P.S. – I changed my name.

Just Another Coincidence

I was president of the local softball association and responsible for arranging the season ending banquet and awards presentations for the boys' league. It was a father and son affair and was held at the local community hall.

We normally tried to arrange for a guest speaker to fill out the evening. They would tell a few tales, answer some questions, and hobnob with the crowd. Ideally there would be a sports connection of some sort and preferably a local angle as well.

I had heard that a sportswriter named Earl McRae lived in a small community close by and hoped I could convince him to speak at the banquet. McRae at the time wrote for the magazine that was included as part of the Saturday edition of the Toronto Star. He went on to do some television, radio, and more newspaper work after that.

Perhaps McRae eventually became best known for his Remembrance Day soliloquy several years back. He recounts how when he was a young boy, a widow took him to her attic and began to show him some war artifacts and uniform pieces that had belonged to her husband before he was killed in action. He provides some detail as to the items she showed him and how fascinated he was by it all.

By the end of the story, McRae reveals who that the fallen soldier was. It was his own father who had made the supreme sacrifice, a father he was too young to remember. The only way he would know anything of him, was through his mother and her memories.

I looked up Mr. McRae's telephone number and gave him a call a few weeks before the banquet. This was in the days before answering machines were commonplace and despite repeated efforts, I either did not get an answer at all when I called, or I ended up speaking to his wife and leaving a message. The game of telephone tag continued and with the banquet only a week away, I still had not spoken to him. I pretty much had given up hope and figured the banquet would have to proceed without a guest speaker this time.

That particular year, I had volunteered to coach a house league hockey team. I wasn't married and didn't have kids of my own playing, but coaching was something I enjoyed. I went to the arena the Saturday morning of the first game of the season and was walking away from the dressing room area, my team having just finished playing their first game.

Keep in mind that I had never met Earl McRae, had never spoken to him on the phone, and would not recognize him if I saw him. The only idea I had of what he looked like, was based on a small picture that sometimes appeared beside the articles he wrote for the Star.

Just as I walked past a group of parents and their hockey-playing sons, on my way to the exit, one of the parents started to introduce himself for the first time to his son's coach. "Hello", he said, "my name is Earl McRae and this is my son."

I stopped in my tracks, turned and politely introduced myself to Mr. Earl McRae. "I've been trying to get in touch with you," I told him. He knew my name, having received the messages I'd left with his wife. He indicated he had also tried to reach me, but had been unsuccessful. After a brief conversation, he agreed to speak at our upcoming banquet.

I look back at this story as one of those things that seemed as if it was just meant to happen, not that it was anything extraordinary.

I wouldn't have known Earl McRae by sight alone. The only way I could hope to recognize him, was if I happened to be in the same place as him, at the same time, and he happened to say his name just as I walked by. That's exactly what happened!

What a coincidence!

The Proposal

Margaret and I had been dating each other for about a year. We had started to talk more seriously about the future. Our dating helped us realize that we had a number of common interests and compatible personalities. We seemed to have similar future expectations and goals.

We both wanted children, two being the ideal number, a boy and a girl of course. We were not the same religion, she was Catholic and I was Protestant, but we were both flexible enough to make that of no concern. She was born in Portugal and raised in Canada by parents rooted in many European traditions. My family was Canadian born and raised, back through a few generations. I was a country boy and she was a city girl. We both had psychology degrees.

I wanted to propose to Margaret, but I also wanted to do it in some sort of unique way.

As a gift to my parent's a few months earlier, I had made a video story of their life. This was before video cameras were quite so common in many households and certainly before they were so compact in size.

Without my parents' knowledge, I had secretly interviewed many of their friends and relatives and made videos of many old family photographs. After much editing, adding some music and voice-overs, the final product was completed and delivered to them. It was something of a keepsake they could pull out and watch every now and then in the years that followed.

With this *creative* production now on my personal resume, I decided that proposing to Margaret on video was what I wanted to do. I set about creating a series of video shots of myself around the house, using a tripod and other accessories as needed.

This time the music I chose was from Jim Croce, a pop/folk singer who had burst onto the scene in the 70's with several top hits, only to die tragically in a plane crash before realizing his full potential. The lyrics to the song on my video were, "… every time I tried to tell you, the words just came out wrong, so I'll have to say I love you in a song."

I invited Margaret over one day and asked her to watch this video I had recently made. I popped it in the VCR and pressed play.

Jim Croce begins to sing his song providing the audio, while the video shows me doing some routine household activities. The song continues to play in the background of the video. As the song begins to come to an end and the video with it, there I am on the screen wearing a large coat.

I remove the coat and have a sweater on underneath. I remove the sweater, and then another sweater, followed by a sweat-top, a shirt and so on. All the while Jim Croce's "I'll have to say I love you in a song" plays on. Finally, after removing several layers of upper body clothing, I'm left wearing a t-shirt, a t-shirt with a sign that says, "Margaret, will you marry me?" I stretch out my arms; palms raised and shrug my shoulders as if to say, "Well?"

She said, "Yes".

I Would Like to Marry your Daughter

So, Margaret had said, "Yes", but her father would have to give his blessing as well. She told me that he wouldn't say no, but because of their traditional Portuguese background, I would have to officially ask him for permission to marry his daughter. I was on good terms with her family and didn't have a problem with this at all.

However, I thought it would be kind of neat if I could learn enough Portuguese to ask the question in her father's native language. Her dad spoke English, but I thought he might be impressed if I could ask for his daughter's hand in marriage in Portuguese.

It just so happened that I worked with a couple of other young Portuguese women at the time. So, I explained the situation to them and asked them to teach me how to say, "I would like to marry your daughter".

They wrote the words out and carefully pronounced them for me. I rewrote them phonetically and practiced over the next few days. The two colleagues provided feedback and finally I thought I was ready.

The day of the *big ask* was rapidly approaching when I started to panic a little. Both of these girls at work were fun-loving and not averse to a practical joke. What if the Portuguese words they had taught me to speak weren't asking what I thought they were asking?

What if in fact, I would end up telling Margaret's father I wanted to do something else to his daughter other than marry her?

These two potential practical jokers could have substituted any number of Portuguese words for the word marry. "Yes sir, I would like to ---- your daughter", I would say with a smile on my face. Yikes, the relationship might end right there!

I did the only thing I could do. I found someone else who spoke Portuguese and I told them I was going to attempt to say something and I wanted them to translate it back to me in English.

Fortunately, all my fears were unwarranted. I was saying what I wanted to say. I said it well enough that Margaret's father understood me.

He said, "Yes", too!

The Mighty Duck Influence

In the 1990's, Disney made a series of *Mighty Duck* hockey movies. They eventually purchased a National Hockey League franchise and assigned it the same moniker. The first *Mighty Duck* movie and those that followed to a lesser extent, were big hits with younger kids. Their themes were always the same; the no-chance underdogs, the team of misfits, somehow defy the odds and win the big game.

Our son, Jeremy, who was four or five years old, had watched the first Mighty Ducks movie several times. I have to admit, I liked those types of films too. They always stressed the importance of the team over the individual. Work together and you'll overcome the odds. Help your teammates and you'll get the best results.

As pre-school kids can tend to do, on one particular day Jeremy had moved from one toy, game or activity to another in quick succession, and after a few hours very little of what he had gotten out to play with had been put away. There were toys and games scattered all around the family room.

I told him it was time to start tidying up and to put his toys back in the toy box.

Did he immediately begin to put things back where they belonged? …. No.

Did he just ignore my request? …. No.

Instead, he turned to me and said, "Dad, we need to work as a team!"

Thank you, *Mighty Ducks*!

Gidget the Dog

What's your favorite pet story?

The family dog we had when my sister and I were children, was part Pekinese and part Toy-Pomeranian. We named her Gidget.

Gidget was like most other dogs I suspect. Once she became familiar with our routines, when we left for work or school and what time we would arrive back home, her own schedule evolved. That would be to sleep most of the time we were away, allow her built-in body clock to wake her a half hour or so before we were due back home, watch for us out the window, and get really excited when we arrived.

Pet owners and non-pet owners alike are sometimes surprised at just how smart an animal can be, especially if it's their own. The animal's instincts often detect when something out of the ordinary occurs and they let their owner know.

If we had guests visiting in the evening and they stayed past the usual bedtime, Gidget would let them know by barking at them. They couldn't understand why the dog that had remained quiet most of the night, was all of a sudden creating a fuss. We knew she was just trying to tell them it was time to leave; both her and our routines were being disrupted.

By the way, one of my uncles had his own way of telling visitors that they had stayed too late. He would bring a manual alarm clock from his bedroom and start to wind it in front of his guests.

Anyway, back to Gidget. One morning after everyone had left the house except my mother, the dog was not herself. Rather than preparing for her daylong nap, she was in the kitchen kicking up a fuss, continually barking. My mother couldn't figure out why. It was almost as if Gidget didn't want her to leave for work.

Finally, mom realized that Gidget was barking at the stove and the reason she was barking at the stove was that a burner had been left on; her way of reminding my Mom to turn it off before she left for work.

I'm sure others have more spectacular stories of dogs warning them of potential danger or even saving a life, but this is a small one of ours.

The Ombudsman

I must admit that I wondered in advance if I would really want this job. After all, what it really was, was *The Complaints Department*. No one would ever bring good news to the office. How would I feel just listening to people complain, especially if there was no validity to their claims?

An ombudsman is someone who is tasked with investigating potentially improper actions by an administration or specific people, quite often ethical in nature. We had an ombudsman position at MDCAN and I filled the role along with my regular analyst duties, for two years.

There ended up being a number of legitimate concerns and the role provided me with some valuable experience.

If employees felt that professional business standards were not being upheld, some moral obligations were not being met or any other ethical boundaries were crossed, they could lodge a complaint with the ombudsman. They could also approach their supervisor, their union steward or a human resources professional. The nature of the issue often determined which route an employee would take, but regardless of which way it went, a level of confidentiality was expected to be maintained.

The ombudsman role at MDCAN did not authorize them to intercede in the normal chain of command. I could explain the results of any investigations that I had completed and make appropriate recommendations. I could not force a decision on a manager or a department where the functional responsibility lay. In my case, I would usually copy a manager's boss to try to ensure that the manager responsible felt some pressure to take the action that I had suggested.

One of the more interesting internal cases that I had to deal with while in the ombudsman role, was a complaint that came from a unionized office worker.

The bargaining unit positions had various salary grades and if a job was posted there was a formal manner in which to apply. The collective agreement allowed for preference to be given to the more senior employees who applied for an opening. However, management also had a right to ensure that the candidates were adequately qualified.

As a result, the policy in place dictated that there would be a written test which was deemed appropriate in measuring the skills required to successfully do the job. Each applicant for the posted position would be required to take the test and of those who exceeded a certain grade (I believe it was 70%), the one with the most seniority would be offered the job. So, the most senior employee who passed the test, got the promotion.

The complaint I received came from an unsuccessful internal candidate for a specific job that had been posted. In this case, two people were required, so based on the one posting two successful candidates were selected.

The test for this particular role was primarily mathematical in nature. The test the manager created consisted of five problems that had to be solved utilizing the required knowledge, doing the analysis and executing the calculations.

The complainant told me that he thought that the supervisor knew who he wanted to get the jobs and he had provided some of the questions to them in advance. This had given them a very obvious and unfair advantage.

He said that there was a mathematics textbook that the supervisor always left on his desk, which was located in an open office area and anyone was free to borrow it from him. Candidates knew that the book contained the types of questions that would be on the test. In this case, it contained some of the actual questions that ended up on the test.

So, the complaint was not necessarily that the supervisor gave the specific questions directly to some candidates, but rather that he sneakily made them aware of where they were in the textbook.

The complainant went on to say that when he looked at the textbook that was on the supervisor's desk, there was a page missing. His own investigation took him to the local library, where he found another copy of

What A Concidence!

the book to try to discover what was on the missing page. Lo and behold, he told me, it contained two of the five mathematical problems that were on the test they had all written.

So, what was being implied was, that the supervisor had told his preferred candidates the exact page that some questions were on, and then either he or one of the candidates, ripped the page from the book. Anyone else who borrowed it, would not be able to study the details of the missing questions in advance.

My own investigation included talking to all of the job candidates and the supervisor. As is the case in many of these types of situations, there were conflicting accounts as to exactly what happened. I was left having to make a decision without solid evidence to guide me.

Five people had written the test and the top two in seniority who had passed, were told that they were the successful candidates. Would it be fair to ask those who had completed the test honestly, and without prior knowledge of any of the questions, to rewrite it? I didn't think so.

On the other hand, there were enough questions in my own mind to acknowledge that something was amiss and it needed to be addressed appropriately. It appeared as though some of the candidates may indeed have had prior knowledge of some of the test questions. As a result, I didn't feel that I could let the results stand.

I decided on something of a compromise. I declared that the marks on the two questions that had been shown to be on the test and also shown to have been on the page that had been removed from the supervisor's textbook, would not count towards any candidate's final grades. The other three problems would count and any other non-mathematical questions would count as well.

It was the only way I could think of to try to make the playing field equal for all, without them having to take a new test.

The order of finish would now change, but guess what? The same two employees who had the highest marks, still had the best scores and they would once again be declared to be the successful candidates. Their ranking was reversed however, with the original first place finisher switching places with the person who had finished second, but that didn't really matter. They both would be moving up a pay grade or two.

The employee who brought the complaint to me was not happy of course. He would not get a promotion. His final mark still fell below the successful candidates.

I felt that despite that, I had come up with a fair and equitable solution. It was accepted and adopted by those in charge.

Fast Forward 15 years

I was now a manager at Humber College. I posted a clerical position for my department. There was a test that was associated with it that involved creating and manipulating an Excel spreadsheet. There were four internal candidates who took the test.

Human Resources had more than one version of this Excel test. I had indicated that only beginner level Excel was required for this position, so that's the one they administered.

Apparently, there were copies of these tests floating around outside of the H.R. department, presumably secretly kept by those who had taken the test previously for jobs posted in the past.

Well, when the results came back for the tests of those who had applied for the job in my area, it was obvious they had gotten their hands on the questions in advance.

How did we know? Well, the beginner Excel test asked the candidates to create a spreadsheet and perform a few basic tasks.

The intermediate test had the candidates perform those same steps, creating the same spreadsheet and then building on it by requiring them to complete more complex tasks.

The advanced version of the test asked them to go even further with the same spreadsheet, demonstrating the use of even more advanced features.

Remember how I said that the basic Excel test was the one given to the candidates for the job in my department?

Well, two of the candidates actually created spreadsheets as if they had been given the intermediate version. They answered questions and performed tasks that weren't even asked of them!

They were disqualified from the competition of course and H.R. changed their method of administering the tests from that day on.

Winner's Circle

Have you ever dreamt about being on a championship team? Maybe you weren't a player. Maybe you had some other role, but there you were in the photo with the rest of the real team, smiling and celebrating a victory.

It was a summer evening in the mid 1970's and a few of us who were working at a hockey school, myself and my cousin James included, decided to go to the local horse races one evening. It was a small harness racing track located in Belleville at the time.

We placed a few bets, won some and lost some. Since we were all in our late teens or early twenties, we didn't have a lot of money to bet anyway.

After each race, the winning horse would be brought back in front of the grandstand near the finish line and the owner's friends and family would parade out onto the track for their photo opportunity. As is custom, they would gather round the horse and the jockey/driver, while the track photographer snapped their picture. We were watching the races from close to the rail that night and had seen this practice repeated after every race.

Usually there would be three, four, maybe even five people somehow connected to the winning owner who would be part of the photo.

After one particular race however, the entourage was as large as I've ever seen. It had to be at least twenty people. There must have been lots of friends and family in attendance and they all began walking past us out onto the track, proud to be associated with the latest winner and to get their photo taken.

James decided to join their group. He followed them out onto the track, took his place beside them, placed his hands behind his back and smiled broadly as the photographer clicked the shutter. He became forever a part of this horse's big victory and we had our biggest laugh of the night.

No one said anything to him. Maybe everyone just assumed he was a friend of someone else in the group or perhaps he was a racetrack official. They must have been really puzzled when they received the printed photo.

Who is this guy to the right side of the picture? I thought he was your friend! No, I thought he was here with you!

50 Things I've learned about My Wife

On the occasion of Margaret's 50th birthday, I gave her this list of the 50 things I had learned about her.

1. She was born in Portugal and moved to Canada when she was 1 year old.
2. She doesn't look her age.
3. She has 4 brothers and 3 sisters.
4. She likes babies a lot.
5. She runs the place, just like every other secretary at a school.
6. She never sneezes just once. It's always a minimum of five.
7. She talks to her mother every day.
8. She's an expert on American Idol.
9. She likes to drink tea, wine, and specialty coffees.
10. She has to pee a lot.
11. Her right leg is very sensitive.
12. She hates all telemarketers who call to try to sell us duct cleaning services.
13. She's afraid of dogs, except for Grizzly & Bailey.
14. She's an expert on The Amazing Race.
15. She's good at crosswords.
16. Rarely does she utter cross words.
17. Her favorite piece of furniture is the couch.
18. She always keeps the house well protected by a thin layer of dust.
19. Her favorite thing in the world is chocolate.
20. She has a very youthful looking neck.
21. She's an expert on Dancing with the Stars.
22. She'll choose a hot tub over a pool 99% of the time.

23. On at least one occasion, she shaved one armpit and forgot to do the other.
24. She usually decides what she's going to cook for dinner about 5 minutes before.
25. She likes bubble baths.
26. She came to Canada on a boat ….. or maybe it was a plane.
27. It took a week ….. or maybe only a day.
28. She doesn't really know how she came to Canada or how long it took.
29. Her two wishes growing up were for a pony and white go-go boots. She got neither.
30. She used to dislike the taste of water.
31. She has to pee a lot.
32. She never has anything to wear.
33. Her second favorite piece of furniture is the bed, for sleeping.
34. She's an expert on Seinfeld.
35. She usually sits at the back and tries to be inconspicuous.
36. She's moved on from Donny Osmond to Josh Groban.
37. She has the millionaire's family - a boy and a girl.
38. She's not a millionaire and she didn't marry one so she'll have to keep working.
39. She's well spoken.
40. She's intelligent.
41. Mornings come too early for her.
42. It takes her a long time to do her hair.
43. She likes to laugh, sometimes uncontrollably.
44. She has to pee a lot
45. She usually chooses the salmon or the chicken.
46. She exercises her leg while sitting.
47. Sometimes, she snorts when she laughs.
48. She walks fast when it's really cold or about to rain.
49. She likes to do things as a family.
50. I'm glad I met her!

Another Difficult Decision

I had a decision to make and it wasn't an easy one.

I was president of the local softball association. I received a call from the parent of a boy who played on one of our Pee Wee Boys House League Teams. The parent said that he thought that one of his son's 12-year-old teammates had been drinking alcohol before the game!

This was a small town where pretty much everyone knew each other. Underage drinking was one thing, but a 12-year-old seemed unimaginable!

I didn't happen to be at the ballpark the previous evening, so I wasn't there to witness anything myself.

I started to call the coaches and talk to some other parents. Many of the coaches of our house league teams were teenagers themselves, so they were only four or five years older than some of their players.

While the boy in question wasn't falling down drunk, there were enough people who said his behavior did not seem normal, that I began to think there was some validity to the report I had received.

I called the boy's mother and told her what I had been told. She confronted her son and he denied everything. He said he definitely had not been drinking.

So, again I had to make a decision with some conflicting stories.

If the boy had been drinking, I needed to take some sort of action. I couldn't let it go with no response. It would be especially important to send a message to him and any teammates who might know the truth, that there were consequences for this behavior.

The easy thing would be to do nothing, while keeping a closer eye on him going forward. Instead, I decided I would suspend him for one month.

I called his mother and told her. She was not happy.

I really did not know if I had done the right thing. I was conflicted before I made the decision and bothered by it afterwards. After all, I may have tried and convicted an innocent boy.

Fast Forward 2 hours

My phone rang. I answered and it's was the boy's mother. He had finally confessed. I breathed a sigh of relief and thanked her. She thanked me too.

The Dream

Kirby and Vi were friends of my parents, not friends that they would see on a weekly basis, but friends that they socialized with regularly and if they hadn't seen each other for a while, they would make sure they arranged to get together in the near future.

Usually, they would meet up at some local social event, perhaps a dance at the Innis Lake Dance Hall or maybe some other locale a little further away.

Kirby and Vi had two children, both boys, while my parents had two kids as well, my sister Diane and myself.

Vi use to have this recurring dream, a dream that she told Kirby about and eventually she told others as well. I guess you'd have to describe it as more of a nightmare, because she used to see her husband in a coffin and there was another smaller coffin beside him. In the dream she would constantly reach to try to see who or what was inside the other coffin, but was never able to do so.

One day Kirby had taken their oldest son with him in the pickup truck and was traveling along a sideroad not far from home that intersected with a branch of the CN rail line. In those days on this road, there were no barriers that would lower to prevent a vehicle from the crossing railroad tracks if there was a train approaching. There were no flashing red lights of warning either. Motorists had to rely on visual checks of their own and the sound of the oncoming train's whistle.

Nobody is sure exactly what happened that day. Perhaps Kirby was distracted momentarily, maybe he didn't hear the train whistle blowing, or maybe the whistle hadn't sounded at all. In any case, the train smashed into the side of the truck, killing both him and his son.

Vi became a widow that day, having lost her husband and oldest son. She now had the answers to some of the questions from that dream she had experienced so many times. They were answers she wished she had never come to know. It was a nightmare that became her reality.

Spell Check

Spell check is great. Autofill is also great. But beware, they both have their drawbacks!

Having software automatically check your spelling and grammar, or complete a word you have just started to type, can prevent you from sending an e-mail off with a lot of errors. It can also save you a lot of time.

However, they do not catch correctly spelled words that you did not intend to type and they do not warn you of missing words.

The first two personal examples of this, I caught before hitting the send button. The third example I did not!

Example 1 - My boss at the time was named Denise. I had many occasions where I would send her work-related emails. The problem was, for some reason every time I started to type "Hi Denise", my computer software would change it to "Hi Dense". Needless to say, calling your boss *dense* could be a career-limiting move. Fortunately, I proofread the emails well enough that I never hit the send button before correcting her name. Phew!!

Example 2 – One of the directors of our finance department was named Sanjay. In this case, whenever I typed "Hi Sanjay", the computer software changed it to read "Hi Santa." As I said many times, if Santa really did work in our finance department, he never would have asked us to cut our budget! Again, I caught this error/typo before actually sending any emails to him.

Example 3 - At the time at Humber College, we had several technologists who only worked 10 months of the year. They would typically be laid off for July and August.

One particular year, there was a special project that a technologist named Ennio was scheduled to work on over the summer months instead of being laid off. I had to complete the paperwork to extend him for the additional weeks of work. I did this and composed an email to send to Human Resources to explain the situation.

The email read something like this. "Our department has a special project we are working on this July and August. As a result, Ennio will not be getting **laid off** this summer. Paperwork reflecting this has been sent in the inter-office mail." Well, at least that is what the email was supposed to say.

A couple of weeks later, I was cleaning up my old emails. I came across the one mentioned above. As I re-read it, I realized I had left a word out of it. I had somehow forgotten to type the word **off**.

I'm not sure if Ennio realized he wouldn't be *getting any* that summer.

The next time I was in the Human Resources Department, I said, "I sent you folks an e-mail a while back and I accidently left a word out of it." Not only had they noticed, they had been passing it around the office so everyone got a good laugh!

Sometimes, There's Nothing You Can Do

I decided to follow the road straight north. It was February and I was on my way home after a recreational game of hockey with some friends, the one we played every Tuesday night immediately after work.

The decision to follow this less traveled road, rather than the highway through more populated areas was a conscious one. It would be a little more relaxing drive as I was unwinding after an hour of exercise.

I passed an intersection with another road that didn't have much traffic and decided it would have been better to have turned there to continue my drive home. So, I pulled over to the shoulder of the road, intending to turn around and go back to make the turn that I'd missed.

The problem was, it was the middle of winter. It was getting dark and there was snow on the side of the road. In fact, there was enough snow to disguise the fact that the shoulder of the road was very narrow. It was so narrow that there really wasn't enough room to pull off the road and as I did so, my passenger side wheels sunk into the ditch.

So now what do I do?

I'm by myself. My car is in the ditch on a country road in the days before cell phones, and there are no houses in sight that I might easily walk to for help.

All it took was about sixty seconds, a minute or maybe even a bit less. A pickup truck came up behind me. It pulled off the road, although not as far as me. The driver got out, asked if I needed some help, got a chain from his truck, hooked it to my car and pulled me out.

Larry Proctor

I couldn't believe the timing, my luck, and the fact that a truck with a driver ready to lend a hand and the chain to do it with, showed up right when and where I needed him. A welcome coincidence to say the least.

The Snowball Letter

George was a retired man in his seventies, a neighbor who kept active and always seemed to have some project on the go around the house.

It was a mild winter day, immediately after a snowfall. It was a snowfall that had left lots of good packing snow on the ground.

George was walking up the street, returning from a trip to a local store when he spotted up ahead of him, another neighbor named Bruce. Bruce had not noticed George who was walking some distance behind him.

George, being a bit of a practical joker, bent over and picked up a handful of snow that he proceeded to form into a snowball. He reared back and let it fly. His aim was good and he hit his surprised target right in the back of the head!

Wiping the snow from himself, the victim turned to face his assailant and to George's horror, it wasn't Bruce! It was a face he recognized from the neighborhood, a face that from that distance had apparently looked a lot like Bruce, but not someone who's name George even knew.

Naturally, George was very apologetic, explaining how he mistook the fellow for a friend and it was all meant to be in fun and he hoped he wasn't hurt and so on and so on.

George recounted the story to a few people including myself over the next few days.

I, along with my wife, who worked at a local school where teachers were constantly having to remind children of the dangers of snowball throwing, decided that George deserved to be reprimanded. He should receive a letter similar to those dispensed to students who broke the rules and threw snowballs at others.

We started with the school letter format as a draft, changed the wording to appear as though it originated from an unnamed town official, added an authentic looking logo, and mailed it to George.

The specifics of the letter pointed out that George's actions were dangerous to other residents of the town, were totally unacceptable, and he was being placed on probation. He was not allowed out of his house after any significant snowfall unless accompanied by his wife. A copy of the letter was to remain posted outside his house, warning any visitors of his antisocial behavior.

George and his wife were going to be moving from the area to another part of the province in the spring, so the letter also stated that if he should ever move from his present location, a copy of the letter would be sent to the town council of their new residence as a warning.

George had forgotten he had told me about the snowball incident so his list of potential perpetrators did not include Margaret and me.

Eventually we decided we had better tell him the truth when we heard that he might be about to wrongfully accuse someone else.

As far as we know, that was the last snowball he ever threw.

A Child's Definition of "Budget"

Occasionally while videotaping our kids when they were young, we'd do a question and answer session with them. Years later, these would prove to be more interesting to watch than the birthday parties, the swimming lessons and the soccer games, although the unorganized/natural play videos can be pretty entertaining too.

There was a British television show at the time, where a host would ask children various questions. I guess it was modelled after the even older American show, "Kids Say the Darndest Things", hosted by Art Linkletter.

Anyway, I decided to interview our kids, asking their opinions on various topics and what they thought certain words or expressions meant.

The most well thought out response to one of my questions came from my nephew, Ryan, when I asked him what the word *budget* meant.

I could tell he was considering his answer very carefully before responding, undoubtedly drawing on some occasion when he had perhaps heard his parents use the word.

He finally said, "It's when you're trying to move a refrigerator and you can't."

This answer really puzzled me, but I finally figured it out. I can picture Ryan watching his Dad exerting himself, trying to move the fridge one day and he just couldn't *budge it*!

Rewind 40 years

I used to ask my Mom and Dad a lot of questions when I was a kid. The one that I'm most proud of, which no matter how much I thought about it,

I could not imagine any logical answer to was, "What did the men stand on to build the ground?"

I mean the ground wasn't there from the beginning of time, right? It had to have been built by someone. And they must have had to stand on something to build it!

Surprise Me

The news the doctor gave them came as a shock. It wasn't bad news though. In fact, it was very good news.

They were both in their early thirties. They had one child, a beautiful little girl who was five years old. They had rewarding careers and a house of their own.

The doc had just informed them that they were both in excellent condition. They lived healthy lifestyles and there was no reason why they couldn't both live well into their nineties. Wow, another sixty years together!

How were they ever going to get through that? Don't get me wrong, they had a great relationship. It's just that, well, sixty years is a long time. I mean it's almost twice as long as they had already been on this planet. How could they keep things interesting for sixty more years? How would they not get bored with one another?

That's the basis for Sophie Kinsella's novel, "Surprise Me".

If you have read the book, you'll know that the couple decides they should each come up with ways to surprise their partner. This wouldn't be just one surprise each. They were free to come up with, and put into action, as many ideas as they could. There were no rules related to how long, how much or when this would all happen.

If you haven't read the book, and not to provide too much of a spoiler, a lot of these surprises, actually most of these surprises, don't work out well. The person being surprised is not nearly as pleased as the one doing the surprising thinks they should be. What one thought the other might really enjoy, was not always the case.

Not only that, what if they both planned surprises for the same time on the same day? What if they were surprises which they had spent a lot of money on?

My wife and I had a similar idea before I read that Kinsella work of fiction.

Our 25th wedding anniversary was upcoming and we went to Niagara Falls for the weekend. The weather was great (we were married in November). We had tickets for a magic show which turned out to be very entertaining, a couple of really nice dinners, and even stopped at a small roadside chapel where we spontaneously renewed our vows, just the two of us.

Margaret said, "I think we should celebrate our anniversary every month". That sounded like a good idea to me, so our version of the surprise date was born.

Each month, we had a date night and we took turns planning those dates. The nature of the date had to be a surprise, but for practical purposes, we had to let each know when it would take place.

Most were for an evening or a half day at most. Once or twice a year however, we would spend a couple of days away. The drive to the date was part of the anticipation too. If I was planning that month's event I would know where we were headed, but Margaret would not, and when she planned things, it was vice versa.

Some months it was just a movie or maybe dinner somewhere special. Other times, it was something we wouldn't ordinarily do.

Paint Nite was Margaret's idea. That was where we were each taught how to create something on canvas while we enjoyed a glass of wine. Her painting was much better than mine, but neither ended up hanging in our house.

A ballroom dancing competition was my idea since Margaret likes "Dancing with the Stars" so much. Just to make it clear, we were spectators only! We did not enter the contest. Besides, my only related experience would have been the square dance exhibition that I was part of at the Bolton Fall Fair, when I was in the eighth grade. Much to my chagrin, I was one of those selected to participate. All the girls wanted to get picked. None of the boys did.

What A Concidence!

Margaret and I had indoor picnics, a cooking class with a prominent chef at a local restaurant, make-believe summer vacations with pina coladas in our family room in the middle of winter and short hikes on local trails.

One of the bigger surprises for Margaret was when I bought theatre tickets for a play in St. Jacobs. I had secretly arranged for a good friend of hers, whom she hadn't seen in over ten years, to be seated right beside us.

The biggest surprise for me was one of the weekends away. I was doing the driving not knowing our final destination, while Margaret provided directions. As we headed towards the Niagara area and then passed it, the U.S. border was fast approaching. "I didn't bring my passport!", I said. Margaret smiled. She had everything under control though, including having packed our passports.

The date ended up being a weekend in Buffalo, with tickets to the hockey game between my beloved Toronto Maple Leafs and the Buffalo Sabres.

A couple of years later, we celebrated another anniversary with a weekend in Montreal. This time it included tickets to a Toronto versus Montreal hockey game.

We arrived on a Friday and had booked a nearby restaurant for dinner. The hockey game would follow the next night.

The restaurant was both intimate and elegant. It was an older house that had been converted to a fine dining establishment with just a couple of relatively small rooms, each containing only six or seven tables.

We had a table for two and there was a larger table in the corner of the room that had six fellows sitting at it when we arrived. I immediately recognized all of them. The Maple Leafs had arrived in Montreal the night before their game and seated at the table were the general manager at the time and the entire coaching staff.

So, even though my wife was sitting right in front of me AND it was our anniversary, I may have spent more time watching the Leaf's coaching staff, paying more attention to what they were saying, than I did to her.

Toothy Art

Later in life my father wore dentures, but for a while he had a removable plate with just one false tooth attached. It was an upper plate and the one tooth was just slightly off the center of his mouth. Is that called an incisor? Anyway, at some point he had something more permanent done and he no longer wore or needed this removable dental plate.

I was in my first year of high school at the time and my mother worked as a secretary in the office of the school I attended. That's an important part of this story.

I was taking a 9th grade art class despite the fact I was not very artistic at all. One of our projects was to create a sculpture, or maybe it's called a mobile, on a styrofoam base. Well, I searched around the house grabbing anything and everything I could find to use for my *sculpture*. As you've probably guessed, I decided to use my dad's false tooth as the centerpiece. After all, he didn't need it anymore.

I don't remember what kind of a grade I received for that project, probably a "C", but I'd prefer to remember it as at least a "B" minus. The sculpture itself didn't mean much to me and it was left with most of the other student's projects on a shelf, or maybe it was in a cupboard in the classroom.

Sometime later, somehow or other, that tooth of my Dad's became dislodged from my project and fell on the floor. Another student found it and decided that whoever it belonged to would probably be missing it, so they took it to the lost and found in the office.

The secretary who took it from the student called my mother over (remember she worked in the office) and said "Jean, look at this, some student has lost their false tooth." My Mom took one look at it and said, "That looks like my husband's tooth!"

Larry Proctor

The main topic of conversation that night at our dinner table was how well Mom knew her husband's body parts, even the false ones.

Bedtime

The routine says the kids go to bed at 8 o'clock, or 9 o'clock, or whatever the time happens to be in your household. The problem is although the parents are ready, the kids never seem to be.

How can we get them ready, make them want to go to bed? Maybe if we make a game of it?

That's what we did in our house when the kids were young. I invented this game called treasure hunt, or scavenger hunt, or find the clue, the name doesn't really matter.

In advance, I prepared a series of clues and directions on scrap pieces of paper and hid them around the house.

The first clue was given to the kids who had to read it, or interpret the picture if they were too young to read. It might say something like, "Go to the television", or just show a picture of a television. They would race off to the television and somewhere in the vicinity, they would find another clue. This one might say, "Go to the refrigerator." Of course, they couldn't wait to get to the fridge. This continued from one piece of furniture to another, from one area of the house to the next.

They would be led around the house over the course of the next few minutes, each time finding another clue. It was a game to them, but something more to us, the parents. You see, it would eventually lead them to their beds.

When they got to the second last clue, they would find themselves in the bathroom and be instructed to brush their teeth.

The last clue would lead them to their bedroom. It also would tell them to pick a book to read and if all went according to plan, they'd fall asleep a short time later.

P.S. – Everything did not always go according to plan.

More Alike Every Day

It's said that the longer couples are married, the more alike they become. Some even appear to look alike, a scary thought for my wife I'm sure!

One day after work, Margaret told me that she had been to a Tim Horton's Drive Thru for lunch that day. After getting in line, she remembered that she had made her lunch, but with no way to get out of line, she decided to order a coffee and a bagel anyway. After paying for her purchase, she did get her coffee, but drove off without the bagel only to realize later that she had forgotten it.

The strange thing is that on the exact same day I had gone to another Tim Horton's, paid for a coffee and drove away without it.

A few days earlier I had come home and said I thought I'd done something to help solve an ongoing problem. The problem of determining which one of us (i.e. – the kids), was consistently forgetting to put their lunch bag ice pack back in the freezer each day. So many were missing. I had purchased different colored ones during my lunch break that day. We would now all have our own identifiable ice packs. Margaret had gone out and made exactly the same purchase the same day unknown to me!

Margaret kept telling me that this particular Christmas she was having trouble coming up with ideas for gifts for me. One day when I was out shopping on my own, I saw a paperback novel I thought I'd like and decided to buy it. I brought it home and gave it to her and said, "Here, this can be a stocking stuffer gift from you to me." We had never discussed this book previously and I thought she'd be happy that this was one less gift she'd have to buy. Then she told me that she had purchased the exact same book the day before.

After leaving the house, I opened the driver's side door to get into our van and proceeded to bang it into my shin. A loud "Ouch" followed. A few seconds later, Margaret opened the passenger door and banged the exact same part of the door into her shin. Her yell was a little louder. We now had matching bruises, except that mine was on the left leg and hers was on the right.

I'm sure that there were more of these types of stories in the past and as I reread them, I see that there's not really much to them, but as we age together, I'm sure there will be more coincidences in the future, hopefully more interesting ones!

To Margaret's relief however, we still don't look very much alike at all!

The Christmas Newsletter

My mother liked to send and receive Christmas Newsletters each year. She loved to hear what people were doing, especially if she didn't see them very often.

She also liked to summarize the events in her and my dad's life as another year came to a close. Describing what had kept them busy over the year was only part of the news she would pass on. She also would let everyone on her list know what had transpired in the lives of myself and my sister. In my case, it would extend to my wife Margaret and our kids, Jeremy and Laura, who of course were my mom's grandchildren.

Each December mom would draft her portion of the newsletter and ask my sister and I to provide something about our lives and families that could be included. Some years, it was difficult to write something new, especially if we were working at the same jobs, the kids were at the same schools, and they were playing the same sports.

I got to thinking how most newsletters, no matter who they were from, seemed to always be very positive. People obviously weren't telling their friends all the news in their lives, only the good stuff. I decided to buck that trend.

This is what we provided one year (tongue in cheek) to my mom for inclusion in her newsletter.

"Larry and Margaret are still together on Larry Street. The kids, Jeremy and Laura, spend their days at school and their nights watching television.

Margaret still works as a school secretary. She spends most of her day applying ice to student's injuries and checking their heads for lice. The school is crawling with lice.

Margaret also lost five pounds recently, but it was mostly from her boobs and her face.

Larry works in Orangeville and has a constant ringing in his left ear. He does surveys and reads the newspaper when he has time.

Prior to starting his current job, he did some part time supply teaching, just enough to realize he wouldn't want to do it all the time. He went to Buffalo anyway, to check out getting his teaching certification from a college there.

Sometimes he has up to four bowel movements in one day! What's really irritating though, is that he's always walking around with the label on his shirt sticking out!

Laura and Jeremy never put their lunch ice packs in the freezer when they get home from school. Three are now missing! Neither kid ever seems to have any homework. The family never invites anyone over because the house is a mess!! The kids are slobs and their parents are slobs!

Merry Christmas and Happy New Year to All!"

Needless to say, it never made it to the newsletter that was distributed that year. I resubmitted something more normal.

Your Favorite Films

I think I've established that whether it be the stories of my life or yours, it is those events, those anecdotes, the ones we can remember, the ones we consider worth repeating and some that we never will, that ultimately define us.

It's not what type of person you tell others you are that determines how they see you. It's not the characteristics you claim to have. It's the actions you take that demonstrate those qualities that we are all judged on. You would only have to relate a few tales to someone for them to start to develop an image of who you are, understand what is important to you and appreciate your beliefs.

It's kind of like your resume. You can say that you're organized and analytical and that you're a team player. Anybody can do that. But, for others to accept that you in fact do have those qualities, you must provide examples that demonstrate it. You have to tell them your stories.

Here's an exercise for you. Ask someone what their favorite movies are. It can be a friend you have known for some time or someone you've just met. I'll bet that based on that alone, you'll start to formulate or reformulate an opinion of them.

Are the films comedies, action movies, thrillers or musicals? Are they a mix of those genres or more?

Did they like the films because the lead character seemed to have some similar characteristics to them OR because they lacked those same qualities, but found them so admirable?

Did the movie remind them of some similar life experience they had in the past or were they nothing like anything they had ever done, but wished they had?

One thing I do find, is that regardless of whether it's music or film, most of us will remember more fondly what we heard or viewed in our late teens and early twenties. That seems to have been our most impressionable time of life. You are more likely to experience new things and get exposed to new ideas at that age.

It takes something really extraordinary later in life to be seen to be better. You've already been there, done that.

The ground rules for my favorite films are that they must have been released during my lifetime. Old classics are excluded. So now here are just some of them, imbedded in a short non-sensical story that I made up, just to accommodate as many as I could.

Before I was able to talk and before I was able to understand what was being said to me, I appreciated *the sound of music*.

As I grew, I began to *witness* many wondrous things. Like any child though, there were ups and downs. Sometimes, the road was *rocky* and sometimes life even felt like it would be one long, *titanic* struggle. At moments like that, it would have been easy to retreat into a *cocoon*.

I could have trouble seeing the *forrest gump* for the trees. I might even have thought I was *one flew over the cuckoo's nest*. But if I ever thought I saw a *ghost*, encountered an *E.T.* or had any other *close encounter of the third kind*, I could always find a way out. It would be *the great escape*.

All of those feelings would *die hard*. Because of that, there was no need for any reclamation, no *shawshank redemption*.

There were never any great riches, no *moneyball* and never any references to being a *slumdog millionaire*. I might *inherit the wind*, but not much more.

I never knew an *Annie Hall* or a *JFK*. I never had any friends I would refer to as *the fugitive* or *raiders of the lost ark*. I never felt *the sting*.

Chariots of fire could inspire me to persevere. Sometimes, victories could even be snatched from the *jaws* of defeat. Occasionally, there seemed to be a *sixth sense* that would confidently point me *back to the future*. Everything was real though. Nobody referred to anything as *the imitation game*.

Ultimately, there was a feeling of contentment. It was the result of many factors no doubt, but *Oh God*, I'm sure at least one of them was *love actually*.

Powerful Image

Some images we never lose. They're imbedded in our minds forever.

When we were young, my sister and I would quite often stay overnight at our grandparents who lived three houses away. If our own parents were going out for the evening, it just made more sense for us to sleep over, rather than them waking us and bringing us home at some late hour.

I usually slept on a couch in a small den. From there, I could see across the hall and down a bit, directly into the bedroom where my grandfather slept.

I can remember having gone to bed and being able to see my grandfather as he headed off to his room. Before getting into bed, he got down on his knees, rested his elbows on the edge of the bed, folded his hands and said a prayer.

Now this is a pose that we may picture for young children. It's not something that I expected to see my grandfather do, a man in his seventies at the time. It's not that I didn't think adults prayed outside of church, but this was an image that I never imagined for anyone other than a young child. It was powerful and symbolic in many ways.

Although a night time prayer may start as something that some parents encourage as a part of their child's daily routine, it doesn't have to end there. For some it may stop in their teens and resume again later in life, but for others it is an integral part of their faith and endures a lifetime.

Now I Understand

Sometimes we never understand the reason why. Or maybe we get it later.

Whenever I would stand beside my father in church and we were singing a hymn, I noticed that on different occasions he would stop singing for a period during the song. Then he would start again and finish with the rest of the congregation. It was almost as if he forgot the words or lost his place in the hymn book.

More than once I noticed this behavior, but I never asked him why this occurred. I think I know the answer now, because since my father has passed, it has happened to me.

If you're like me, and I'm like my father in many ways, during a church service the mind can wander. Sometimes I'm hearing the minister or priest's every word. Other times I'm off in another world of thought.

Occasionally the words I'm hearing or the thoughts I'm having, whether they are as a result of what's being said or because of the place I'm at in my life, they initiate an internal, emotional response. This reaction can be happy or sad, distressing or thankful, as I reflect on a particular moment in life. Whatever the case, the emotions can be strong enough to choke a person up. They can be strong enough to stop someone singing for a while.

Longevity

My Uncle Ted slowly cut the meat on his dinner plate, picked up a piece with his fork, and chewed it well before swallowing. He repeated this with the potatoes, vegetables, and anything else on his plate until it was clean. Eventually he finished his meal, the last of us to do so. He didn't talk much while eating. He let others do most of that. Those of us who found a way to talk and eat also found a way to do so quickly.

If someone asked me to mention one defining characteristic about Ted, it would be how slowly and methodically he ate his meals. Come to think of it, he was always active and he did most things thoroughly and methodically. Ted is still going strong in his late 90's.

My grandmother also lived well into her 90's. She grew up on a farm, raised her seven children and went to church almost every week. If I had to remark on one defining characteristic about her, it would be how hardworking she had been for her entire life. She looked after many of the farm chores and almost all of the child-rearing duties, while my grandfather was trying to get a trucking business established.

My mother similarly has lived into her 90's. She was also raised on a farm, cooked most of her meals from scratch, rarely ate processed foods and kept learning new things as she aged. While many of her age who were retired didn't bother much with personal computers when they became commonplace, mom was not afraid of the new technology.

As a bit of an aside, my mother, believe it or not, has three kidneys. I doubt this has had any effect on her longevity though.

So, maybe eating slowly, doing some physical labor for at least part of your life and keeping your mind active might all contribute to building a sound mind and strong body. We can probably add to that some of the obvious things, like a balanced diet, good sleeping habits, and regular exercise to increase the chances of a long life.

My wife, Margaret, was listening to a podcast a few years ago. It was done by someone who had studied longevity in humans. The gerontologist had found a small village in Italy where almost everyone knew each other. This village had a much higher life expectancy than most, so the gerontologist set out to determine why.

The Mediterranean diet might be the answer, but there were many other settlements whose diets were virtually the same, yet their residents didn't live as long.

This village had more of a personal touch to it. They all knew each other. They all looked out for one another. Anyone who wasn't a close friend or relative was at least an acquaintance.

Just saying "Hello" to someone you pass on the street can have an extremely beneficial effect on your mood, which in turn of course can positively affect your health and well-being. You don't have to even know the other person's name. The dog walkers you cross paths with regularly, the coffee shop lady who knows your order, and even the parking lot attendant who recognizes your face, but knows nothing else about you.

I was someone who liked to get into work early. As such, I was often one of the first in my assigned parking lot each day. I would usually wave hello at the attendant as I entered the lot.

One day, I pulled up to the entrance and he didn't lift the barrier to allow me to drive into the lot. I thought maybe he couldn't see my parking pass, so I took it off the visor of the car and held it up to the window. He still didn't lift the barrier. Finally, I opened my driver's side window. He leaned out of the window of the parking booth and said, "You usually wave at me every morning and today you didn't." I smiled up at him, waved and he let me in.

I think that was an example of the daily greetings, acknowledgements or whatever else you want to call them, that we all need in some form or another. Of course, we need close, personal relationships, but the casual ones are important too.

P.S. – Shortly after retiring I joined a local fitness center and as part of my new routine, I worked out there 3-4 mornings a week. I got talking to another member who was older than me one day and told him I had recently retired.

He gave me a solid piece of advice. He said, "Retirement is a good thing, but you have to work at it."

Throughout our busy working lives, we dream about eventually having some laid-back, do little days that retirement can bring. However, we still need some sort of plan and some sort of routine, and just as importantly, some casual day-to-day interaction with others to aid in both our long term mental and physical well-being.

What Does the Future Hold?

I once saw a video which explained some of the views of a futurist named Joel Barker. Predicting what might be a good investment or what direction you should channel your career or even just having the foresight to do and say the things that will make your life more rewarding, is not always the easiest thing to do.

We can read and analyze many different ideas, observe current trends, and armed with as many facts as are available still make the wrong decision.

Futurists are really trying to do what everyone else is, project the future and make the corresponding right choices today based on current trends.

We never know what our future holds, but we can certainly be as observant as possible and maybe we'll pick up some clues.

One of the stories that this particular futurist told, was of a man who loved cars and on a Sunday afternoon liked nothing better than to take a sports car of his out for a drive in the country.

One particular weekend he was doing what he loved, enjoying a beautiful sunny day while cruising along a country road. He felt connected to the vehicle he was driving, completely in tune with it and was experiencing a feeling of elation that he often had on days like this.

The gentleman Sunday driver approached a curve in the road and as he rounded the corner, all of a sudden out of nowhere appeared a large SUV. The SUV was crossing the center line. It was on the wrong side of the road, his side!

It required a split-second, life-saving reaction by the man in the sports car, who until then had been thoroughly enjoying his leisurely Sunday drive. He quickly turned the wheel of his car, took to the shoulder of the road and managed to avoid what might have been a catastrophic collision. As he did that, the driver of the SUV yelled out her window to him, "Pig!"

How dare she call him a name! She was on his side of the road! How infuriating, but once again his reaction was quick. He shouted right back at her, "Cow!" That provided him with some degree of satisfaction. He had managed to respond to her insult with one of his own, and he was pretty sure she had heard him.

His face was red with anger, his heart was pounding and he was still gripping the steering wheel tightly, but he got his car back on the pavement and continued round the bend. As he came out of the curve he looked straight ahead, but it was already too late. He ran head on into a pig! A pig that was right in the middle of the road!

Sometimes we ignore the warning signs that might help guide us into the future and sometimes we simply misinterpret them.

Some of our life experiences just seem to be too much of a coincidence to not have some special meaning to them. Others we don't recognize the relevance of until we look back on them years later. In the end though, it's that collection of personal stories that help define us as individuals and give our lives meaning.

Towards the end of the movie Forrest Gump, Tom Hanks playing the title character, is reflecting on the twists and turns his own life has taken, just like that feather in the same scene that is being blown around in the wind.

He says, "I don't know if we've got a destiny or if we're just floating along on a breeze. I think it's probably a little of both."

Conclusion

There is a certain randomness to life, but there are also those coincidences we've all encountered, which led us to believe that some things were just meant to be. The events we remember the best, coincidence or not, and the stories we tell the most are the ones that are likely to define us as individuals.

I took a social psychology course in my second year of university. It turned out to be one of the most interesting courses I ever took. The professor was an excellent speaker and a great story teller. He seemed to have an intriguing tale to tell for almost every lecture topic that we studied.

When choosing my courses for third year, I noticed another social psychology course taught by the same professor, so I quickly signed up for it. Guess what? That professor told the same stories in that class that I had already heard the previous year. What a disappointment!

So, in the same way that I tell and retell my own stories to friends, be forewarned. If there is ever a sequel to this book, it'll probably contain all of the same tales this one does.

About the Author

Larry Proctor has lived all of his life in Caledon, Ontario. He continues to live there with his wife, Margaret. They have two grown children. His family roots in Caledon go back to his great grandfather and when Larry was an infant, his grandfather named a street after him.

Larry is now retired. His primary employment was initially with McDonnell Douglas Aircraft which later merged with Boeing. The last 11 years prior to retirement, he worked as a Business Manager at Humber College.

Printed in Canada